大学英语立体化网络化系列教材·拓展课程教材

英美文化与习俗

British and American Cultures and Customs

主　编　焦　英　钱　清
主　审　解又明

图书在版编目(CIP)数据

英美文化与习俗/焦英,钱清主编.—北京:北京大学出版社,2009.8
(大学英语立体化网络化系列教材·拓展课程教材)
ISBN 978-7-301-15623-0

Ⅰ.英… Ⅱ.①焦…②钱… Ⅲ.①英语-高等学校-教材②英国-概况③美国-概况 Ⅳ.H31

中国版本图书馆 CIP 数据核字(2009)第 133149 号

书　　　　名:	英美文化与习俗
著作责任者:	焦英　钱清　主编　解又明　主审
责 任 编 辑:	张建民
标 准 书 号:	ISBN 978-7-301-15623-0
出 版 发 行:	北京大学出版社
地　　　　址:	北京市海淀区成府路 205 号　100871
网　　　　址:	http://www.pup.cn　新浪微博:@北京大学出版社
电 子 邮 箱:	编辑部 pupwaiwen@pup.cn　总编室 zpup@pup.cn
电　　　　话:	邮购部 62752015　发行部 62750672　编辑部 62759634
印　　刷　者:	北京虎彩文化传播有限公司
经　　销　者:	新华书店
	650 毫米×980 毫米　16 开本　13 印张　190 千字
	2009 年 8 月第 1 版　2024 年 6 月第 6 次印刷
定　　　　价:	39.00 元

未经许可,不得以任何方式复制或抄袭本书之部分或全部内容。
版权所有,侵权必究
举报电话: 010-62752024　电子邮箱: fd@pup.cn
图书如有印装质量问题,请与出版部联系,电话: 010-62756370

前　言

　　要想学会一门外国语言,必须了解产生、使用这种语言的特定的社会文化背景;否则,就不可能真正掌握这门语言。了解外国文化背景知识不仅有助于学生提高阅读理解水平,培养学生跨文化交际的能力,也可以使学生在认识和了解西方社会文明的过程中,逐步地提高个人的文化素质和修养。

　　"英美文化与习俗"课程旨在让学生通过大量的篇章阅读,扩大文化背景知识,深入了解英美文化、社会习俗与我国文化和习俗之间的差异。在学习过程中不断地增强语感,提高语篇的理解能力;同时让学生通过对所读文章内容的分析、归纳、判断理解,不断地提高英语语言的实际应用能力。选修该课程的学生在授课老师的指导下,通过篇章阅读、课堂讨论、个人陈述、测试、问答等各种形式的课堂活动和语言训练,打下较扎实的语言基础,养成自主学习的好习惯,并有助于提高英语的综合应用能力。

　　"英美文化与习俗"课程也可以为那些准备出国深造的学生提供一个了解西方文化、礼仪、习俗的平台,帮助他们能够更快地适应异国的生活与学习环境。

　　本教材共分为六个单元:1.社会风俗与习惯;2.社交礼仪与礼节;3.生活方式与风格;4.食品与饮食习惯;5.传统节日及其历史;6.体育竞技与娱乐消遣。其内容贴近生活,语言规范。其中的文章都选自英美原文,内容丰富;注重了趣味性、知识性和实用性。每单元由多篇文章构成,每篇文章500—2000字不等。在每篇文章之后提供了一些篇章理解的思考题以及讨论题。这些练习可以在老师的指导下开展个人陈述、小组讨论等交互式的课堂活动;自学者也可以通过这些习题检测个人对所读文章的理解情况。本书最后附有一套测试题,帮助学生检查自己的学习结果。

本书的教学对象主要是在校的大学生,也可以作为备考英语三级的学习者的英语读物。我们希望这本书能成为读者掌握和应用英语的好帮手。

编者

2009年1月

Contents 目录

Unit One   Customs and Habits 社会风俗与习惯 / 1
1. Hi, Folks 嗨,伙计 / 1
2. How Titles Are Used 如何使用头衔 / 4
3. Reasons for Being Informal 举止随意的原因 / 6
4. Concept of Privacy 隐私的概念 / 9
5. Thanks and Apologies 感谢与道歉 / 12
6. What We Do When Invited 被邀请时做什么 / 15
7. Ladies First 女士优先 / 18
8. Small Talk 小话题 / 20
9. Misunderstanding 误解 / 22
10. Three Threes in Britain 英国的"三三"习俗 / 24

Unit Two   Manners and Courtesies 社交礼仪与礼节 / 31
1. The Way of Expressing Courtesy 表达礼貌的方式 / 31
2. Bringing Gifts 携带礼物 / 33
3. Behavior in Public Places 公共场合的举止行为 / 36
4. Table Manners 餐桌礼仪 / 46
5. Campus Social Relations 校园内的社会交往 / 57

Unit Three   Life Styles and Patterns 生活方式与风格 / 64
1. Pace of Life 生活节奏 / 64
2. Friendship Patterns 友谊模式 / 66
3. Housing 住房 / 70

  4. Finding a Rest Room 寻找厕所 / 86
  5. Driving 开车 / 87
  6. The Americans Living in the Suburban Houses 住在郊区的美国人 / 94
  7. Leisure and Private Life in Britain 英国人的闲暇时光和私生活 / 97

Unit Four Food Customs and Eating 食品与饮食习惯 / 102
  1. Food Customs 饮食习俗 / 102
  2. Traditional English Food 传统的英国食品 / 110
  3. Dining with Americans 与美国人共餐 / 115

Unit Five Holidays and Their Histories 传统节日及其历史 / 119
  1. New Year's Day, January 1st 新年(1月1日) / 119
  2. April Fools' Day 四月愚人节 / 127
  3. The Easter Symbols 复活节的象征物 / 132
  4. Traditional Halloween and Halloween Changes 传统万圣节和万圣节的变化 / 136
  5. The Thanksgiving History and Modern Thanksgiving Day 感恩节的历史和现代感恩节 / 140
  6. Christmas, December 25th 圣诞节(12月25日) / 147

Unit Six Sports, Recreation and Entertainment 体育竞技与消遣娱乐 / 157
  1. Sports 体育竞技 / 157
  2. Recreation 消遣 / 168
  3. Entertainment 娱乐 / 176

Test Paper 课程试题 / 191
Answers 答案 / 200

Unit One
CUSTOMS AND HABITS

> Fast modern airplanes seem to have made the world a much smaller place. With increasing frequency, people travel from one country to another to conduct business or just to visit. Many visitors to the United States, in particular, find that customs and habits in America are quite different from those observed in their own countries.

1. Hi, Folks

I think the first thing you ought to know about American customs is how introductions are made in the States. The great difference between American social customs and those of other countries lies in the way in which names are used. Most Americans don't like using Mr., Mrs. or Miss. They find these terms too formal. In the States, people of all ages may prefer to be called by their first names. For example, one may say, "My name is Wilson. James Wilson. Call me James." "Glad to meet you. I'm Miller. But call me Paul." A lady that you meet for the first time might say, "Don't call me Mrs. Smith. Just call me Sally."

So, you see, addressing people

by their first names usually indicates friendliness. Very often, introductions are made by using people's first or last names; for example, "Mary Smith, this is John Jones." In this situation, you are free to decide whether to call the lady "Mary" or "Miss Smith". Sometimes both of you will begin a conversation by using family names, that is, surnames (Mr. Smith; Miss White) and after a while one or both of you may begin using the first names instead. Of course, foreigners who come to the States may feel uncomfortable of using only the first names. For them it is quite acceptable to be more formal. A person may just smile and say, "Excuse my being formal when I meet new friends. I am accustomed to it. After a while I'll use their first names." If American friends do not use your last names or titles, that really doesn't mean any lack of respect. They are used to being informal. I can give you another example of their informality. Yesterday, some members of an American delegation and I came across a few American tourists here in Shanghai. One of the tourists asked, "Hi, folks, where from?" "Los Angeles," answered one delegate member. So you can see how informal we Americans are.

The use of "nicknames" is fairly common among people in the United States. A nickname is not the person's real name but a name assigned to him or her because of certain physical characteristics, behavior patterns, or some other factors. Foreign students often get nicknames if their names seem too long or unpronounceable to their American friends. Being called by a nickname is not usually uncomplimentary; on the contrary, it may indicate that the student is viewed with respect and even affection.

Words and Expressions

1. frequency /'fri:kwənsi/ n. the repeated or frequent happening of something 经常性；频繁性

Unit One Customs and Habits

2. **conduct** /kənˈdʌkt/ *v.* to do, direct or lead 经营；管理；引导
3. **observe** /əbˈzɜːv/ *v.* to obey or follow a custom; to celebrate 遵守习俗；(正式)举行仪式或庆祝
4. **lie in** (*phrasal verb*) to remain or be kept in the stated condition or position; to locate 在于；位于
5. **term** /tɜːm/ *n.* a word with a special meaning 专用名词；术语
6. **indicate** /ˈindikeit/ *v.* to show or point to something 表示；表明
7. **after a while** (*a phrase*) after a period of time 一会儿；一段时间
8. **be (become, get) accustomed to** (*phrasal verb*) to be (get) used to 习惯于
9. **informality** /ˌinfɔːˈmæliti/ *n.* in a way of being friendly and relaxed or suitable for not serious situation 非正式；不拘礼节
10. **come across** (*phrasal verb*) to meet someone or find something that one does not expect 偶遇
11. **assign** /əˈsain/ *v.* to give as a share or for use 分配；分给
12. **unpronounceable** /ˈʌnprəˈnaunsəbl/ *adj.* unable to be pronounced 无法发音的
13. **uncomplimentary** /ˈʌnˌkɔmpliˈmentəri/ *adj.* not expressing admiration, praise, respect, etc. 无法恭维的；不能称赞的
14. **affection** /əˈfekʃən/ *n.* gentle, lasting love or fondness 爱情；深情；喜爱

Content Questions

1. What is the great difference between American social customs and those of other countries?
2. What names do Americans prefer to use when they address each other? And why?
3. What names do American people like to use when they are introduced to each other?
4. How do foreign visitors feel when they are called only by their first names?
5. What is the American characteristic displayed in this passage?

A Question for Thinking and Discussion

How do Chinese differ from Americans in using names?

2. How Titles Are Used

In addition to Mr., Mrs. and Miss, there is one more term, Ms, which is becoming more and more popular in the United States. Ms is used either for a married woman or unmarried woman. So when you are not certain whether to call the lady "Miss" or "Mrs." you may just call her Ms. But be sure that the four terms, Mr. Mrs. Miss and Ms, are followed by the last names.

When you first meet an American and want to be respectful, you can always use "sir" or "madam" in place of their names. The person you address (so) will probably realize that you are not sure of the proper title to use and will help you by telling you the correct term.

However, you'll find formal titles very seldom used in the United States, except in some special occupations—judges, high government officials, certain military officers, medical workers, doctors, professors and religious leaders. Most of these titles are followed by surnames. For example, Judge Harley, Senator Smith, General Clark, Dr. Brown (medical), Dr. Green (professor), Bishop Gray. But for a professor, who is nearly always a university professor, you may call him professor, with or without his surname.

One more point about "sir" and "madam." They are not followed by either the first names or the last names. Don't say "Sir

Ford," "Madam Smith" except when "sir" is used as the title of a knight or baronet in England, e. g. Sir John. His wife is addressed as Dame or Lady Smith.

"Sir" and "madam" show respect for position and seniority, but there is some slight difference in actual usage. For instance, at school, students address their man teacher "sir," but seldom address their woman teacher "madam".

In China, I often hear students address their teacher "Teacher Wang," "Teacher Li." This is not practiced in the United States. And administrative titles like director, manager, principal, dean, chancellor, etc. are not used as forms of address.

Words and Expressions

1. **title** /'taitl/ *n.* a word used in front of a surname to show one's profession, rank, etc. 尊称;头衔
2. **address** /ə'dres/ *v.* (*formal*) to speak to someone or call someone or something 称呼(正式)
3. **Ms** /miz/ *n.* a word used before a woman's name 女士(专用名词)
4. **in place of** (*a phrase*) instead of someone or something 代替;替代
5. **occupation** /ˌɔkju'peiʃən/ *n.* a job or profession 工作;职业
6. **bishop** /'biʃəp/ *n.* an important and high ranked priest 主教
7. **knight** /nait/ *n.* a man of high rank in the Middle Ages while riding a horse 骑士;武士;勇士
8. **baronet** /'bærənit/ *n.* a member of noble ranking below baron (英国的)从男爵(世袭)
9. **dame** /deim/ *n.* (title of a) woman who has been awarded the highest grade of the Order of the British Empire (古)夫人;贵妇人
10. **seniority** /siːni'briti/ *n.* high rank or position in an organization 地位高的;资格老的
11. **actual** /'æktʃuəl/ *adj.* exact or real 真实的;确切的

12. **administrative** /əd'ministrətiv/ *adj.* executive; managing 行政上的;管理的
13. **principal** /'prinsəpəl/ *n.* a person in charge of a school, a schoolmaster (中、小学)校长
14. **dean** /di:n/ *n.* the head of academic faculty 院长;系主任;教务长
15. **chancellor** /'tʃɑ:nsələ/ *n.* a high government official; the head of a university 政府首脑;(大学)校长

Content Questions

1. Why has "Ms" become a more popular term to address a woman?
2. What titles do you use to show your respect for people?
3. When are formal titles used to address people?
4. What titles do Americans use without being followed by surnames?
5. For what purpose do people use "sir" "madam"?
6. What titles are rarely used in the U.S. as forms of address?

A Question for Thinking and Discussion

What is the difference between Chinese and Americans in using titles?

3. Reasons for Being Informal

Often you see men working at office desks without their suit coats and ties. They may lean far back in their chairs and even put their feet up on the desk while they talk on the phone. But this is not meant to be rude. They are informal, most likely because they are always in a great hurry; city people always appear to be hurrying to

Unit One Customs and Habits

get where they are going and would be very impatient if they are delayed even for a brief moment.

But when they discover that you are a stranger, most Americans will become quite kindly and will make a point of helping you. If you need help or want to ask a question, choose a friendly looking person and say, "Excuse me, I am a stranger here. Can you help me?" Most probably, I believe, he will stop, smile at you, and help you find your way or answer  your questions. Occasionally, you will find the person too busy, too rushed to give you aid. Please do not be discouraged. Just ask someone else. And most Americans are especially friendly to Chinese. So if you go to the United States and are in need of help, do not hesitate to ask for it.

There is one more point I'd like to tell you so that you will not misunderstand the Americans when you visit the United States. When you have just got acquainted with an American, he may ask you: "Where do you work?" "How many children do you have?" "How large is your house?" or "Have you had a vacation yet?" Such questions are considered too personal in Europe and are not supposed to be asked if two people are not on very close terms. But Americans do ask such questions to learn what they may have in common with you or just in order to begin a conversation.

This is also the way that Americans themselves become familiar with one another. Because people move from place to place in the United States so often, this type of asking questions has become the normal way that they get to know the many new people they meet. In some countries, it may take a very long time before a visitor is asked questions about personal subjects, such as his family, job, or home. Because things move much faster in the United States,

Americans do not have the time for formalities. They must get to know you today because in a short time they may move to another city far across the country.

Words and Expressions

1. **lean** /liːn/ *v.* to rest against something, or rest something against something else 依靠；倾斜
2. **make a point of** (*phrasal verb*) to do something in a very deliberate or obvious way 明确表示(刻意)要做
3. **too rush to give aid** (*a phrase*) too busy to offer a person a help 太忙而无法给予帮助
4. **hesitate** /ˈheziteit/ *v.* to wait slightly before you do something 犹豫；踌躇
5. **get (be) acquainted with** (*phrasal verb*) to get to know someone or something 熟悉；了解
6. **be on (close, good, bad) terms with someone** (*a phrase*) to have a (close, good, bad) relationship with someone 与某人……(关系密切,关系好,关系不好)
7. **have (little, much, something) in common with** (*a phrase*) to have the same interest, experiences, tastes, etc. as someone else 与某人……(没有多少,有许多,有一些)共同点

Content Questions

1. How do Americans behave in their office?
2. What are the reasons for Americans being informal?
3. What suggestion does the author give to the Chinese who are in need of help in the United States?
4. What questions do you usually avoid asking in Europe but you needn't do so in America?
5. How do Americans get familiar with one another?
6. Why do Americans have no time for formality?

Unit One Customs and Habits

A Question for Thinking and Discussion
How do Chinese usually behave and act in the office?

4. Concept of Privacy

However, there are still quite a few questions which you are not supposed to ask even in the United States. It is considered impolite to inquire a person's age, marriage, status, income, religious belief, choice in voting, and other aspects of privacy. It is, therefore, advisable to get familiar with the American idea of personal privacy before going to the States, for people in China might have quite a different concept.

In order to understand the American, or Western idea of personal privacy, you should start by thinking of a nation's concept of "territoriality." A nation has borders or boundaries, and everything within those boundaries belongs to that nation and no other. And so is it in the case of a private house. If one enters a private house without asking for permission, he is likely to be accused of trespassing or even burglary.

And there is, again, individual territory, even in a house: a person's bedroom, for example, is his or her territory. Those who do not live in that bedroom must not enter without permission and must not open the closet, desk or drawer in that room. On the top of the desk, there may be letters, business papers or other articles.

You must not pick up one of these and read it. If a person is reading something, you must not lean over his shoulder to "share" it with him. It is his private property.

The same concept is true in the office. If it is somebody else's office, always ask, "May I come in?" and wait for an affirmative answer before entering the room.

In the United States, one's income is the top secret. People working in the same office have the faintest idea of how much each person earns, except the boss.

It is also considered impolite to inquire about one's property. If one of your American friends shows you something that he has just bought, you will, of course, say, "What a nice skirt. It looks fabulous." or something like that, but don't inquire about its price.

In the United States, one must not ask about people's age. If you do, they will feel unhappy, especially ladies, young and old. Americans hate to find they are getting old. If an American lady tells you about her age, you may say, "Oh, dear me! You don't expect that I believe you." or "No, really you don't look it."

Words and Expressions

1. **concept** /ˈkɔnsept/ *n.* notion 概念；观念
2. **privacy** /ˈpraivəsi/ *n.* personal life or details unknown to other people 隐私
3. **inquire** /inˈkwaiə/ *v.* to ask for information 询问，打听，咨询
4. **It is advisable... to do something or that** (*a phrase*) It is wise or desirable to do something 做……是明智的
5. **territoriality** /ˌteriˌtɔːriˈæliti/ *n.* land that belongs to a particular country or organization 领土；领地
6. **border** /ˈbɔːdə/ *n.* the place where two countries meet 边境；国界
7. **boundary** /ˈbaundəri/ *n.* the limiting and dividing line between spaces, countries, etc. 疆界；边界

Unit One Customs and Habits

8. **in the case of** (*a phrase*) an example of a situation, or a legal, business problem 在……事例、案例中；在……情形、场合下

9. **be accused of** (*phrasal verb*) to say that someone has done something wrong or illegal 指控；谴责

10. **trespass** /ˈtrespəs/ *v.* to go onto land or place owned by someone without permission 擅自进入；侵入

11. **burglary** /ˈbəːgləri/ *n.* the crime of entering houses or buildings by force with the intention of stealing 盗窃；夜盗

12. **property** /ˈprɔpəti/ *n.* something that one possesses or owns 所有物；财产

13. **affirmative** /əˈfəːmətiv/ *adj.* saying yes, making sure 肯定的；确定的

14. **faint** /feint/ *adj.* difficult to see, hear, know, etc. 不清楚；模糊的

15. **fabulous** /ˈfæbjuləs/ *adj.* extremely good or beautiful 极好的；绝妙的

Content Questions

1. What questions are you supposed not to ask people in America?
2. What is a nation's concept of "territoriality"?
3. What will happen if a person enters a private house without permission in the United States?
4. What are considered individual territories in the West?
5. When you are in someone's bedroom, what shouldn't you do?
6. What is thought of as an impolite question in America?
7. What do you avoid asking when you meet a lady?
8. What will you do even if a lady tells you about her age?

A Question for Thinking and Discussion

What is the contrast between the Westerners and Chinese in the concept of privacy?

5. Thanks and Apologies

As the American people's concept of being polite is different from that held here, I'd like to discuss now the use of "please," "excuse me" and "thank you." I have noticed that the Chinese people use "please" as often as we do on most occasions. But on some occasions they don't use this word. For instance, Chinese teachers rarely say "please sit down" when their students have answered their questions and the traffic police here are also not accustomed to using "please" when they are on duty. At the dinner table when you want some salt, you say "please pass me the salt" instead of stretching out your arms to reach for it. So never forget to say "please" whenever the situation requires it if you are in the States.

I believe we say "excuse me" more often and on more occasions than the Chinese people. We say "excuse me" when we need to pass

in front of someone, to leave a party or the dinner table or when we want to excuse ourselves from company or find ourselves late for an appointment and so on.

"Thank you" means that you appreciate what someone has done for you very often, very small and most ordinary things. So we in the West thank people all day long. For instance, you will thank the saleswoman after she has attended to you. You will say "thank you" to

Unit One Customs and Habits

the waitress when she brings you a cup of coffee. You will say "thank you" to the cashier when you have paid for your food and got your change. And a teacher will say "thank you" to a student who has just answered the question. At home, the husband will thank the wife when she brings him a glass of water. The wife will thank the husband if he helps her with her chair. As the Chinese customs are somewhat different, some Chinese students abroad may appear not polite enough. Very often, they neglect to express thanks for the small favors that others have done for them. On the other hand, however, some Chinese students make excessive expressions of gratitude, which gives us, Westerners, the sense of empty thanks and insincerity, and makes us feel uncomfortable. For example, if an American advisor has spent half an hour helping you edit some letters, you will, of course, want to say, "Thank you, I really appreciate your time (or your help)." That's enough. If you go on and on with statements of thanks, and even add "I'm sorry to have wasted so much of your time.", you will be embarrassing the American. He will feel himself not thanked but annoyed and will not be anxious to help you again. And if he gets really annoyed, he might say, "Well, if you really think that you are wasting my time, you had better stay out of my way." Overdoing apology actually is an awkward behavior in the American society, even if it is done only to be polite. There is also no need for you to apologize for your not being able to speak good English wherever you go and whomever you meet. You must also stop saying that you don't know anything about your specialty.

  You certainly know something that American scholars don't know. So please say what you mean and mean what you say.

Words and Expressions

  1. **apology** /əpɔlədʒi/ *n.* statement of expressing regret for doing something wrong or hurting someone's feelings 道歉；赔不是

2. **stretch** /stretʃ/ *v.*
   to move one's body or part of the body as far as one can 伸展
   to make something become bigger or looser 扩展
3. **company** /'kʌmpəni/ *n.* a person or people who are with you 同伴
4. **appreciate** /ə'priːʃieit/ *v.* to be grateful for something 感激
5. **attend to** (phrasal verb) to serve, to take care of 为……服务；照料
6. **cashier** /kə'ʃiə/ *n.* a person who takes the money when a customer pays for items 收款员；收银员
7. **somewhat** /'sʌmhwɔt/ *ad.*
   to some extent 在某种程度上
   a little; rather 一点；几分
8. **neglect** /ni'glekt/ *v.* not to give enough attention or care to someone or something 疏忽；忽略
9. **favor** /'feivə/ *n.* something that one does to help other people 恩惠；好事
10. **excessive** /ik'sesiv/ *adj.* too much, more than needed 过多的；过分；极度的
11. **gratitude** /'grætitjuːd/ *n.* the feeling that one wants to thank someone for his help or for doing something 感激；感激之情
12. **insincerity** /ˌinsin'seriti/ *n.* not having the quality of being sincere 不真诚；非真心
13. **advisor** /əd'vaizə/ *n.* a person who tells someone what he should do 指导人；忠告者
14. **stay out of one's way** (*a phrase*) to stay away from one's place 别妨碍；别挡道
15. **awkward** /'ɔːkwəd/ *adj.* uncomfortable; uneasy; difficult to deal with 令人难堪的；棘手的
16. **specialty** /'speʃəlti/ *n.* the thing that one knows most about and is best at 专长；特点

Unit One Customs and Habits

Content Questions

1. Which words are often used to show politeness in the Western countries?
2. On what occasions do Americans use "excuse me"?
3. For what purposes do the Westerners use the words "thank you"?
4. Why will an American teacher get annoyed when a Chinese student makes excessive expressions of gratitude?
5. What is considered an awkward behavior in the American society?

A Question for Thinking and Discussion

What is the big contrast in Chinese and the Westerners' expressions of thanks and apologies?

6. What We Do When Invited

Americans often plan social gatherings on short notice, so don't be surprised if you get invited to someone's home or to see a movie or a baseball game without much warning. If the time is convenient for you, by all means accept their invitation. But if you are busy, do not be afraid to decline the invitation, perhaps suggesting a time that would be better. Your host will not feel insulted.

If a friend has invited you to drop in by anytime, it is best to call before visiting to make sure it is convenient for them. Do not stay too long, since you do not want to overstay your welcome.

If you are willing to accept an invitation, you must make it a point to inquire about the day of the week, the date, the time, and the place. If you don't know the way to the place, be sure to ask for instructions.

If later you find that you cannot attend, you should telephone the host or hostess and explain why you cannot come. You should inform your hostess as far ahead of time as possible, because she may wish to invite someone else in your place.

If you have accepted the invitation, you should get to the place at the fixed time, or ten minutes after that. If you happen to be earlier than expected, you had better wait. As the United States is a "do-it-for-yourselves" country, the hostess is likely to be also the cook. She may be busy cooking until the last moment. And she may have no time to change her clothes until five minutes before the party begins and will certainly not be very happy if the guests find her in a mess.

And if you are likely to be 15 minutes late, you should make a telephone call to your hostess. But you must have a proper reason for being late.

If you are invited to attend other activities, such as cocktail or tea parties, or a dance, the time will be somewhat like "5:00 to 7:00 p.m." Then you are free to arrive any time within the hours.

In the United States, people are keenly aware of time and, as a result, Americans tend to organize their activities by means of schedules and are usually on time for business meetings and social activities. Indeed, some visitors from other countries have come to the conclusion that the U.S. society is "ruled by the clock." So, if you go and work or study there, please be punctual.

On your arrival at the party, you may present some flowers to your hostess. But it is not necessary to do so, except on some special occasions, such as birthday, Christmas, New Year and so on. Then, if you are going to stay overnight or over the weekend, it is customary to bring the hostess a small present, often a book, a box of candy, a bottle of wine, or some other similar gift.

Words and Expressions

1. **by all means** (*a phrase*) definitely or certainly 尽一切方法；一定；务必
2. **decline** /di'klain/ *v.* to refuse, to reject 拒绝；谢绝
3. **insult** /in'sʌlt/ *v.* to speak or do something rudely or offensively 侮辱；凌辱
4. **drop in** (*phrasal verb*) to visit someone when he or she is not expecting you 随便拜访一下
5. **overstay** /ˌəuvə'stei/ *v.* to stay too longer 待得超过……限度
6. **instruction** /in'strʌkʃən/ *n.* act or action of teaching or advising 指导；指示
7. **inform** /in'fɔːm/ *v.* to tell or give information 告知；通知
8. **in a mess** (*a phrase*) in a state of disorder 混乱一片
9. **punctual** /'pʌŋktjuəl/ *adj.* arriving at exactly the time that was arranged 准时的；严守时刻的
10. **overnight** /ˌəuvə'nait/ *ad.* for a whole night or during the night 整夜；夜里
11. **customary** /'kʌstəməri/ *adj.* habitual; in agreement with or according to custom 习惯的；风俗的

Content Questions

1. What do you usually do when you are invited by an American friend?
2. What do you have to keep in mind when you drop in an American friend's home?

3. What will you do then if you are willing to accept the invitation?
4. What will you do if you cannot attend a party or a dinner to which you are invited?
5. What is the proper time that you should get to the place where you are invited?
6. Why do you have to be punctual to a dinner or a home party?
7. What do you have to do if you are likely to be 15 minutes late?
8. On what occasions do you have more freedom to arrive at a place where you are invited to?
9. Why is the United States society described as "ruled by the clock"?
10. What is a proper gift that you should take to the hostess?

A Question for Thinking and Discussion

Is there much difference between Americans and Chinese in the customs of accepting an invitation?

7. Ladies First

The host usually shows the guest upon his arrival to the sitting room. If the guest is a lady, most men in the room will stand up when she comes in. Women of all ages still appreciate this courtesy, although the custom is followed by fewer people now than in the past, especially among the younger generation.

In the United States, as in Europe, you will see men usually open doors for women, and women generally walk ahead of men into a room or a restaurant, unless the men have to be ahead of the ladies to choose the table, to open the door or a car or render other services. On the street, men almost always walk or cross the street on the side of the ladies which is closer to the traffic. But if a man walks with two ladies, he should walk in-between them. Then if the host or hostess or both of them come in a car to fetch

their guest for dinner, the guest should squeeze into and sit at the front seat and leave the rear seat vacant, as the host or hostess is also the driver.

Well, let's come back to our dinner party. Suppose when the hostess enters the sitting room with a man guest and sees her daughter there, she will say, "Jane, I'd like you to meet Mr. Wang from China. Mr. Wang has come on an exchange-student program, or something like that." (Here, I assume that the daughter is Jane and the guest is Mr. Wang.)

So, you can see, a man is introduced to a woman, unless he is much older and more senior. As a general rule, younger ones are introduced to elder ones. The ladies in the sitting room will not stand up whether the new comer is a man or a woman.

Words and Expressions

1. **courtesy** /ˈkəːtisi/ *n.* very polite behavior 殷勤；礼貌
2. **render** /ˈrendə/ *v.* to do, show, or furnish 给予；提供；致使
3. **squeeze** /skwiːz/ *v.* to press each side of something with hands or tools 挤；压
4. **rear** /riə/ *adj.* in or at the back of 后部的；后面的
5. **vacant** /ˈveikənt/ *adj.* empty; not occupied 空的；未被占用的

Content Questions

1. What are men expected to do when a woman guest comes into the sitting room?
2. How do good-mannered men in the West behave in public?
3. Where should the guest sit if the host or hostess or both of them come in a car to fetch him/her for dinner?
4. What rules do people have to follow when a new comer is shown into the sitting room?

A Question for Thinking and Discussion

What is the difference between Americans and Chinese when people are introduced to each other?

8. Small Talk

Many Americans find silence uncomfortable during a buffet or a formal dinner. So in the States there is a widespread practice of making "small talk" in certain social situations. Small talk deals with various topics superficially simply for the sake of keeping a conversation going. The topics might include the weather, sports, college courses, clothing, food, etc.. Small talk is especially useful at social gatherings when you meet someone for the first time, or when polite conversation is expected but no serious discussion is desired.

It is common but not necessarily expected that one knows someone in a group before engaging with him or her in conversation. However, at a party or other informal social gathering, a simple "May I join you?" and a self-introduction is normally sufficient to gain acceptance into a group and to join in a conversation. In some places, such as the lobby of a concert hall or theater, a waiting room or a classroom, it is common for strangers to start a conversation even without an introduction. Despite the informality that pervades the U.S. society, people in the States expect those whom they speak to put aside whatever they are doing and listen. As a rule, the conversation distance between two people is at least two or three feet. Standing at a closer range will make many Americans feel uneasy.

Words and Expressions

1. **superficially** /ˌsjuːpəˈfiʃəli/ *ad.* on the surface; insignificantly 表面地;肤浅地
2. **engage with** (*phrasal verb*) to make someone to take part in an activity or talk 使……参加;使……卷入其中
3. **sufficient** /səˈfiʃənt/ *adj.* enough 充分的;足够的
4. **pervade** /pəˈveid/ *v.* to be present throughout 遍及;渗透
5. **put aside** (*phrasal verb*) to set aside or leave for special purpose 放在一边;储存……备用
6. **at a (close) range** (*a phrase*) within the limits of one thing and another 在(靠近的)范围内

Content Questions

1. Why do many Americans prefer to make small talks in certain social situations?
2. What topics would American people like to choose in their small talks?
3. What is the polite way to engage oneself in a conversation?
4. Where can a stranger start a conversation without making a self-introduction?
5. What are the general rules that you have to follow when people speak to you?

A Question for Thinking and Discussion

Do we Chinese have small talks like the Americans? If we do, what topics do we usually have?

9. Misunderstanding

Here I must put in a few words about my experience here in China. If I have dinner with a Chinese host, he always presses more food onto my plate as soon as I have emptied it of the previous helping. That often makes me feel very awkward. I have to eat the food even if I don't feel like it, because it is considered bad manners in the West to leave one's food on the plate. I have also noticed that when a Chinese sits at, say, an American's dinner party, he very often refuses the offer of food or drink though he is in fact still hungry or thirsty. This might be good manners in China, but it is definitely not in the West. In the United States, it is impolite to keep asking someone again and again or press something on him.

Unit One Customs and Habits

Americans are very direct. If they want something, they will ask for it. If not, they will say, "No, thanks." Here's an example: When an American is offered beer by the host, and he doesn't like beer, he will probably say, "No, thanks. I just don't feel like it. I'll take some Diet Pepsi-Cola if you have it." That is what an American will do. Americans consider it confusing to avoid telling the true facts, even if avoiding the truth is done only to be polite. Americans are taught that "Honesty is the best policy." But in  some countries, courtesy might be more important than honesty. That is where misunderstanding occurs when people from two different countries meet. So when I am here in China, I have to observe the customs here. But when you go to the United States, you had better "do as the Romans do."

Words and Expressions

1. **previous** /ˈpriːviəs/ *adj.* happening or coming earlier in time or order 之前的；早先的
2. **Diet Pepsi-Cola** Pepsi-Cola without sugar in it 健怡百事可乐
3. **Honesty is the best policy.** (*a proverb*) 诚实才是上策。
4. **Do as the Romans do.** (*a proverb*) 入乡随俗。

Content Questions

1. Why does a foreign visitor feel very awkward when the Chinese host presses more food on his/her plate?
2. What is considered bad manners at the dinner table in the West?

3. What is the usual reaction of a Chinese when offered more food or drink at a dinner?
4. What is thought of as impoliteness in the United States?
5. What are the typical characteristics of Americans?
6. What is Americans' concept of honesty?
7. Why does misunderstanding often occur when people of different cultures meet?
8. What advice does the author give to the Chinese who come to work or study in America?

A Question for Thinking and Discussion

What is the fundamental difference between American and Chinese attitudes towards honesty and courtesy?

10. Three Threes in Britain

Three "don'ts"

The British have the queue habit. If you have watched a TV news program about Britain or have seen an English film, you probably know of the people lining up one after another, going into the bus, getting on the train or buying something, such as a newspaper. There is seldom any jumping the queue. If somebody jumps up the queue, the British people look down upon him or her. They think that he or she is ill-bred, and take a remarkably dim view of such behavior.

In England, you should never ask a woman about her age. Women do not like others to know their ages. They think it is very impolite of you to ask this question.

Don't try to bargain in Britain when you do the shopping. The

British do not expect or welcome bargaining. Sometimes they consider it losing face. If it is a question of some expensive artwork or a large quantity of antique furniture or silver, you might try to work out a sensible over-all price with your salesman. The British people seldom bargain, they just buy what they want at what they think a reasonable price, and take such a practice for granted.

Three "ings"

Three "ings" refer to betting, drinking and tipping, the ending for each of which is "ing."

The British people are great lovers of betting. They bet mainly on horse racing and Bingo. The former is a gambling sport, the latter a betting game. It is estimated that the total amount staked on all forms of gambling exceeds £2,000 million, or one twentieth of all earnings: £900 million on horses, £250 million on dogs, £300 million on Bingo, £100 million on football pools, and most of the rest in casinos. This is a reduced figure. In 1976, the amount exceeded £8,000 million. The number of people who took part in betting was up to 39 million.

Drinking is another habit of the British people. Most men have the habit of drinking beer, wine and so on. There is another drinking, the drinking of tea. The British drinking habits are severely regulated. The licensing laws, which came into being at the end of the World War I and have continued in existence, govern the operating hours of all cocktail lounges, pubs, inns and liquor shops. Restaurants, too, can sell alcohol at only these hours. The drinking period is usually from 11:30 a.m. to 3 p.m. and again from 5 p.m. to 10:30 p.m., but the hours vary in different localities. The British have also become accustomed to tea-drinking. Every day there are two twenty-minute tea breaks, one in the morning, the other in the afternoon, during which people stop their work and drink tea. Some factories have tea rooms for workers. It is said that the British are the biggest tea consumers, and use up a quarter of the world total of tea production.

Tipping is another custom which the British have. As elsewhere in the West, the tip depends on the type and extent of the service you have received. In some hotels, a service charge of 10 to 15 percent will be added to your bill. Even so, you might want to give something extra to the porter who carries your bags, especially in a first-class establishment. The tipping system in Britain or in the West, consists of small extra payment of the tenth or eighth of the price or bill, given to certain employees, chiefly to waiters, taxi-drivers, hotel servants and railway porters. Apart from these special cases, gifts of money are given only cautiously. This is because the offer of money makes an act of kindness seem like a mean desire for gain.

Three Royal Traditions

Playing the flute is one of the royal traditions. Every morning after breakfast, the Queen listens to the playing of a flute by the royal flutist who does so outside the dining-hall for a quarter of an hour. This is a tradition inherited from Queen Victoria.

The changing shift of the Queen's guards is another of the royal traditions. There are two places in which the ceremonies take place. One ceremony is in front of Buckingham Palace. The other is at Whitehall. Both take place at eleven a. m. weekdays and at ten on Sunday. The Queen's guards, dressed in red coats and black trousers, a white belt, in white gloves, with a glittering sword on the waist and a tall black fur hat on the head, hold this colorful military ceremony before Buckingham Palace. The daily ceremony of the changing shift of the household cavalry guards appears in front of the Horse Guard building.

The third royal tradition involves only the monarch. Annually, the British Queen makes a parliamentary speech, the ceremony for which is rather solemn. She starts out from Buckingham Palace in a brilliant carriage and arrives at the Palace of Westminster by the side of the Thames. When she is seated on the throne in the House of Lords, she sends a messenger with a black walking stick in his hand to the House of Commons on the other end of the Palace to inform them of the Queen's speech. But the gate of the Commons is always closed. When he gets there, he knocks at the door three times with his stick. After the approval of the Speaker, the guard opens the gate and lets him in, and he conveys the Queen's words and bows to the Speaker. Then the Speaker leads all the members of the House of Commons to the House of Lords and attends the speech.

Words and Expressions

1. **queue** /kju:/ *n.* forming a line 排队
2. **line up** (*phrasal verb*) to stand in a line 排成一列;排队
3. **jump the line (queue)** (*a phrase*) to go ahead of people who have been in line longer than you have 排队时加塞儿,插队
4. **ill-bred** *adj.* ill-mannered 教养差的;没有教养的
5. **take a dim view of** (*a phrase*) to show contempt upon 蔑视
6. **bargain** /'bɑːgin/ *v.* to argue with someone and try to reach an agreement, especially on price 讨价还价;谈判
7. **antique** /æn'tiːk/ *n.* a valuable old object or piece of furniture 古董;文物
8. **sensible** /'sensəbl/ *adj.* reasonable 合理的
9. **take something for granted** (*a phrase*) to accept a fact of 认为……是理所当然的;习以为常的
10. **Bingo** /'biŋɡəu/ *n.* a card game 一种用纸牌搭成方块的赌博游戏
11. **estimate** /'estimeit/ *v.* to judge approximately the value, worth, or significance of 估计;评估
12. **stake** /steik/ *v.* to have something wagered 押赌注;把……押下打赌
13. **gambling** /'gæmbliŋ/ *n.* the activity of risking money in an

attempt to win more 赌博

14. **exceed** /ikˈsiːd/ *v.* to be bigger, better, or more than something 超过；胜过

15. **casino** /kəˈsiːnəu/ *n.* a place where people try to win money by playing games 赌场

16. **severely** /siˈviəli/ *ad.* very badly or seriously 严重地；尖锐地；猛烈地

17. **regulate** /ˈregjuːleit/ *v.* to be controlled by rule, law, method, etc. 使……成规则；按规定做

18. **come into being** (*a phrase*) to become something 成型

19. **in existence** (*a phrase*) being real and present 存在

20. **lounge** /laundʒ/ *n.* a room for people to sit or wait 休息室

21. **liquor** /ˈlikə/ *n.* a strong alcoholic drink 烈酒

22. **alcohol** /ˈælkəˌhɔl/ *n.* a substance in wine, beer, etc. 乙醇；酒精

23. **locality** /ləuˈkæliti/ *n.* area; place 地区；地方

24. **consumer** /kənˈsjuːmə/ *n.* someone who buys and uses things 消费者

25. **tip** /tip/ *v.* to give someone a small extra amount of money for a service 付小费

26. **first-class establishment** the best and powerful organization 一流的服务性企业

27. **apart from** (*a phrase*) not included, except 除了

28. **cautiously** /ˈkɔːʃəsli/ *ad.* carefully to avoid danger or trouble 小心地；谨慎地

29. **mean** /miːn/ *adj.* unkind and cruel 刻薄，残酷

30. **flute** /fluːt/ *n.* a musical instrument 长笛

31. **inherit** /inˈherit/ *v.* to get property or money from someone who has died 继承（财产）

32. **the changing shift** a group of soldiers who starts work as another group finishes duty 换岗；倒班

33. **Buckingham Palace** a place in which the Queen of England lives 白金汉宫

Unit One Customs and Habits

34. **Whitehall** /ˈwaitɔːl/ *n.* a place where British Government works 白厅(英国政府所在地)

35. **glitter** /ˈglitə/ *v.* shine with small points of light 闪闪发光

36. **household cavalry** troops on horseback or in armored vehicles 卫队；御林军

37. **monarch** /ˈmɔnək/ *n.* one person who rules a country, such as a king or a queen 君主(国王、女王)

38. **annually** /ˈænjuəli/ *ad.* lasting for only one year, covering the period of a year 每年；一年一次；年度

39. **parliamentary** /ˌpɑːləˈmentəri/ *adj.* of parliament 议会的

40. **solemn** /ˈsɔləm/ *adj.* grave, serious 严肃的，刻板的

41. **brilliant** /ˈbriljənt/ *adj.* very bright, clear and strong 辉煌的；灿烂的

42. **the Palace of Westminster** 威斯敏斯特宫(英国伦敦)

43. **the Thames** England's chief waterway, winds from the Cotswolds to its North Sea estuary 泰晤士河

44. **throne** /θrəun/ *n.* official seat for a king, queen or bishop to sit on 宝座；御座

45. **the House of Lords** upper house of the British parliament 上议院(英国)

46. **messenger** /ˈmesindʒə/ *n.* someone who takes massages or packages containing business papers to people 信使；送信人

47. **inform of** (*phrasal verb*) to tell someone about something 告知；通报

48. **The House of Commons** lower house of the British parliament 下议院(英国)

49. **approval** *n.* something one thinks is good and right 赞成；同意；批准

50. **convey** /kənˈvei/ *v.* to transmit; to send (something) to 传递；传送

51. **bow** /bau/ *v.* to bend one's body forward as a sign of respect or thanks 鞠躬

Content Questions

1. Why do British people look down upon a person who jumps the queue?
2. Why don't the British try to bargain when they do shopping?
3. What do the three "ings" refer to?
4. What do British people like to bet on?
5. Why are the British drinking habits severely regulated?
6. Why are the British said to be the biggest tea consumers?
7. How much will a person tip those who offer service to him?
8. What are the three royal traditions?

A Question for Thinking and Discussion

What can we learn from this passage about the customs of the British? Is there any difference between the British and Chinese in their characteristics and behaviors?

Unit Two
MANNERS AND COURTESIES

1. The Way of Expressing Courtesy

In the United States, you can feel free to visit in people's homes, share their holidays, enjoy their children and their lives without feeling obliged to continue a lifetime relationship. Do not hesitate therefore to accept invitations from Americans simply because you cannot invite them to your home in return. No one will expect you to do so; they realize that you have traveled a great distance. Americans will enjoy welcoming you and will be pleased if you accept their friendship easily.

Visitors may notice that although Americans include them easily in their personal daily lives, they do not show visitors a great amount of special courtesy if doing so requires much time. This is frequently the opposite of what occurs in some countries, where people are especially generous in giving their time to visitors, but do not necessarily welcome them as guests in their homes. In some places, hosts will go to airports late at night to meet a visitor they do not even know well; they spend much time  acting as a guide—all evidence of great generosity. Yet they may never invite the guest to meet their families or join in their family life. It is important to note that in both cases the feeling is equally warm and friendly; only the way of expressing courtesies is different.

Americans warmly welcome visitors into their homes, and try to do as many special things for a guest as time permits. If possible, they will meet you at the airport but if not, you can take public transportation from the airport to your hotel; and taxi or bus from your hotel to their home. Upon arrival, a warm welcome will await you. Indeed, visitors are readily invited into homes during the time they are in the country. Although it may be considered more proper to entertain a guest at a restaurant in some countries, this is not the case in the United States. Generally, however, Americans consider it more friendly to invite a person to one's home than to take him to a restaurant. For purely business purposes, you are more likely to be invited to a restaurant.

Words and Expressions

obliged /ə'blaidʒd/ *adj.* having the obligation to do something 有责任的；有义务的

Content Questions

1. What can you feel free to do when you stay in the U.S.?
2. When Americans welcome you, they don't care whether you will show your courtesy in return. Why?
3. What do Americans usually do if courtesy requires much of their time?
4. What do you have to do if American friends cannot come to meet you at the airport?
5. What is the common way for Americans to entertain a guest?

A Question for Thinking and Discussion

How do Americans differ from the people in some other countries in their way of expressing courtesy?

Unit Two Manners and Courtesies

2. Bringing Gifts

Although it is always welcome, it is not necessary to bring flowers or a gift when you are invited to lunch or dinner, except on special occasions, such as a holiday. Should you wish to bring something, it should be small and simple. If you are going to be an overnight or weekend guest, however, it is customary to bring the hostess a small present—often a book, a box of candy, a bottle of wine, or some similar gift.

In Britain, small gifts such as a pen or a book would be suitable tokens of genuine gratitude and flowers or wine/champagne suffice to thank (junior) colleagues for their services. Do not, however, appear patronizing or unduly forward (especially if the recipient is a woman).

Alternatively, it will often be appreciated if you invite your hosts, or others you wish to thank, out for a meal or to the theatre/opera.

If you are invited to a British home, it is standard practice to bring wine, flowers, and/or chocolates for your hosts. Do not feel offended if the host does not open your gift of wine that evening but adds it to his cellar; it does not mean that the gift is unappreciated but quite simply that he or she has probably already chilled the white wine and opened the red that are appropriate for that meal.

Champagne, though, is never unwelcome and can always be put quickly in the fridge for an after-dinner toast.

Spirits, on the other hand, are a matter of personal taste and best not given as a present. A bottle of your favorite bourbon may languish unopened in the drinks cabinet for years.

The usual European caveats apply when giving flowers: no red roses, white lilies, or chrysanthemums.

If you know that you are going to stay with a family, it is a good idea to bring something from your own country. Your hosts are letting you into the intimacy of their home, so a coffee-table book about your area or some artifact that typifies it would constitute a way of letting your hosts into some of the secrets of your own home. If you are unprepared, then your time in your hosts' house should allow you to think of something they would really appreciate even if you have to mail it from home on your return.

Whenever you have been a guest in a home, you should definitely send a hand-written thank-you note. Indeed, it is a thoughtful gesture to thank your hosts in writing for any hospitality, even after a short drinks party.

Words and Expressions

1. **token** /ˈtəukən/ *n.* a thing that you give to someone to show your feeling 感激的物品
2. **genuine** /ˈdʒenjuin/ *adj.* real and not pretended 真正的；真诚的
3. **suffice** /səˈfais/ *v.* to be enough 足够
4. **patronizing** /ˈpætrənaiziŋ/ *adj.* acting as if better or more important than 神气十足的；以恩人自居的
5. **unduly** /ˌʌnˈdjuːli/ *ad.* improperly 不适当地
6. **recipient** /riˈsipiənt/ *n.* receiver, a person receiving something 接受人；接收人
7. **alternatively** /ɔːlˈtɜːnətivli/ *ad.* (of two things) that may be had or used in place of something else 两者选一；其他
8. **offend** /əˈfend/ *v.* to make someone feel angry and upset 冒犯；得罪

Unit Two Manners and Courtesies

9. **cellar** /'selə/ *n.* underground room, used especially for storing food 地窖；地下室
10. **fridge** /fridʒ/ *n.* (*a short form of the word refrigerator*) a piece of electrical equipment used for storing food at a low temperature 电冰箱
11. **spirit** /'spirit/ *n.* liquor, strong alcoholic drinks 烈酒
12. **bourbon** /'bə:bən/ *n.* whiskey made from corn（玉米酿制的）威士忌酒；波旁威士忌酒
13. **languish** /'læŋgwiʃ/ *v.* to be or become weak 变得衰弱无力；失去活力
14. **cabinet** /'kæbinit/ *n.* a piece of furniture with a door, shelves and drawers where one keeps dishes, knives, forks, etc. 柜橱
15. **caveat** /'kæviæt/ *n.* warning 要求停止行动的警告
16. **apply** /ə'plai/ *v.* to be suitable or right in a particular situation 适用；适合
17. **lily** /'lili/ *n.* a plant with large flowers 百合花
18. **chrysanthemum** /kri'sænθəməm/ *n.* a flower which blooms in fall 菊花
19. **intimacy** /'intiməsi/ *n.* closeness, friendliness 亲密；密切
20. **artifact** /'ɑ:tifækt/ *n.* object made by human being or other beings 人工制品；制造物
21. **typify** /'tipifai/ *v.* to make something have the qualities and features that you would expect 使……成典型
22. **constitute** /'kɔnstitju:t/ *v.* to make up; form 构成；组成
23. **thoughtful** /'θɔ:tful/ *adj.* always thinking about others' needs and feelings 关心他人的；体贴的；考虑周到的
24. **gesture** /'dʒestʃə/ *n.* a movement of one's hand, arm, head to show one's feeling 手势；姿势
25. **hospitality** /ˌhɔspi'tæliti/ *n.* friendly treatment to guests or visitors（对客人的）亲切招待；款待

Content Questions

1. On what occasions do you have to bring a gift to the host or hostess?
2. What is a suitable gift that you should bring to a hostess if you are going to stay overnight or for a weekend?
3. What is the proper way of expressing your thankfulness to (junior) colleagues?
4. What will you never do especially if the recipient of the gift is a woman?
5. Which flowers are not suitable ones as gifts according to the usual European caveats?
6. What will you do whenever you have been a guest in a home?

A Question for Thinking and Discussion

What is the difference between Chinese and the Westerners in bringing gifts to a host or hostess?

3. Behavior in Public Places

When they are out in public—on sidewalks, in stores, restaurants, or in an audience—foreigners are constantly reminded that they are indeed foreigners. This is not just because the people around them differ in color, stature, and language, but also because the other people behave in unfamiliar ways. People's behavior in public places, like

Unit Two Manners and Courtesies

their behavior anywhere else, is subject to cultural influence. The American belief in equality, individuality, and progress are incorporated in the informal rules they follow in public places. Aspects of their communicative style are also evident when they are out in public.

Voice Volume

Words on a page cannot describe how loud sounds are. Suffice it to say that when they are in public places, Americans are generally louder than Germans or Malays, but not as loud as Nigerians or Brazilians. Of course, the volume at which people speak when they are in public places varies from one sort of public situation to another. The crowd at a baseball game will make more noise than the audience in a theater, for example. Patrons in a fast-food restaurant are likely to be noisier than those in a fashionable restaurant.

Foreign visitors who do not want to draw attention to themselves by their unusual behavior will want to note how loudly others around them in public places are talking, and adjust accordingly. Talking more softly than the Americans will cause no problems, but making more noise than they do will draw attention and, perhaps, adverse comment.

Touching

Americans' general aversion to touching others and being touched is clearly evident in public places. The "keep to the right" rule (see below) is one means of reducing the likelihood that strangers will have physical contact with each other.

Americans will rarely crowd onto a bus, train, or other conveyance the way Japanese and Mexicans are famous for doing. They will simply not enter situations where extensive and prolonged physical contact with strangers is unavoidable. Pushing one's way through a crowd is considered quite rude. When they are in a situation where physical contact is unavoidable, Americans will typically try to draw in their shoulders and arms so as to minimize the amount of space they occupy. They will tolerate contact on the outsides of their arms when their arms are hanging straight down from their shoulders, but contacts with other parts of the body make

them extremely anxious. When they are in a tightly crowded situation, such as a full elevator (lift) or bus, they will generally stop talking or will talk only in very low voices. Their discomfort is easy to see.

In cases where they bump into another person or otherwise touch the other person inadvertently, they will quickly draw away and apologize, making clear that the touch was accidental. "Excuse me," they will say, or "Sorry."

Foreign visitors who violate Americans' notions concerning touching, in public places and elsewhere, are likely to be regarded as "pushy" or "aggressive."

Keep to the Right

When they are walking on sidewalks, in hallways, or on stairways—wherever groups of people are walking in two opposite directions, Americans stay on the right side. This enables them to pass each other without physical contact and to progress as quickly as possible.

Line up, and Wait Your Turn

When they are in situations where a group of people want attention or service from someone, Americans line up (or "queue," as some people say). In the bank, at the theater box office, or at the university registrar's counter, the latest person to arrive will step to the end of the line and patiently (patiently unless it becomes clear

Unit Two Manners and Courtesies

that the service the people in the line are getting is slower than it ought to be) wait their turn. This behavior reflects their notion that all people are equal, in the sense that no one has the privilege of going directly to the front of a line. It also reflects their aversion to touching, which is much less likely to happen in a line than in a crowd jostling to get service.

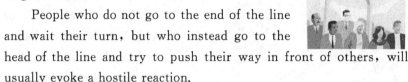

People who do not go to the end of the line and wait their turn, but who instead go to the head of the line and try to push their way in front of others, will usually evoke a hostile reaction.

First-come, First-served

Related to the "line up" rule is the first-come, first-served rule. The general notion is that the person who arrives first gets attention first. Alternative notions, such as giving priority to older people or richer ones or males, do not normally occur to equality-minded Americans.

If several customers are standing up to a counter awaiting service, the clerk might ask, "Who's next?" An honest reply is expected.

Don't Block the Traffic

Generally, Americans give priority to people who are moving rather than to those who are stationary. A person who is in a moving crowd (on a sidewalk, for example) and who wishes to stop or to go more slowly than others is expected to move to the side or otherwise get out of the way of those who are continuing to move. It is considered inconsiderate to obstruct other people's paths.

Don't Block the View

It is also deemed inconsiderate to obstruct another person's view when the person is trying to watch a public event, such as a parade, athletic contest, or eater performance. People toward the front of an audience or crowd are expected to try to position themselves so that people behind them can see. This rule can be interpreted as yet another manifestation of Americans' assumptions about equality and individualism.

Manners of Introduction and Farewell

People often shake hands after being introduced to each other in other countries. In the United States, there may also be a

handshake, if it is formal. But very often the two would just smile and say "Hi" or "Hello," rather than use a more formal handshake. And if they do shake hands, and one of the two sides is a lady, it is preferable for her to reach out her hand first. Otherwise, the gentleman will just keep his hand behind him. And, as a rule, the senior reaches his hand to his junior and the host reaches his to his guest. When shaking hands, men have to take off their gloves, but ladies can do it with their gloves on. Then, when an American leaves a party or a business meeting, he does not usually give a special "fare-well" or handshake to each person; he will often just wave good-bye to the whole group or perhaps say, "Well, so long everybody, I'll see you tomorrow." So they leave without handshakes.

Smoking

A chapter on Americans' behavior in public places must discuss cigarette smoking. This chapter concludes with some words on that topic.

"I never thought much about when and where I smoked when I was at home," a German scholar said. "But here I notice that people look at me unpleasantly if I light a cigarette in a bus or in the restaurant. Several people have even asked me to put out my cigarette!"

In recent years an anti-smoking movement has made

considerable headway in the United States. The results are many. Some states and localities have outlawed smoking in certain public places. Some restaurants, like airplanes, have areas designated for smokers and for non-smokers. Some localities prohibit smoking anywhere inside a restaurant.  Many organizations have formulated rules about smoking, usually rules that specify where people can and cannot smoke. Non-smokers who feel discomfort in the presence of cigarette smoke often ask smokers (or tell them) to extinguish their cigarettes. Large numbers of Americans who formerly smoked have discontinued doing so, and vigorous campaigns in the public schools are aimed at discouraging young people from taking up the habit. People who do smoke are likely to postpone having a cigarette until they are in a situation where they can smoke without "polluting" the air around non-smokers.

Many foreign visitors, like the German scholar, come to the United States from countries where a higher portion of the people smoke and where what many Americans call the "right" of non-smokers to a smoke-free environment gets little or no attention. Such visitors, if they smoke without regard to local laws or non-smokers' sensitivities, are likely to give offense and be regarded as inconsiderate or worse.

Foreign visitors who smoke and who wish to avoid offending Americans will want to notice, before they light up, whether others in the group are smoking and, if they are, whether they are confining themselves to a particular part of the room or building. Asking those around them, "Do you mind if I smoke?" is a good idea, and so is acceding to the wishes of those who say they mind.

Words and Expressions

1. **constantly** /ˈkɔnstəntli/ *ad.* unchangingly; fixedly / 不变地；固定地
2. **stature** /ˈstætʃə/ *n.* a person's natural height 身高；身材
3. **to be subject to** (*a phrase*) to be governed by someone or something else; not independent 受制于；隶属于
4. **incorporated** /inˈkɔːpəreitid/ *adj.* shared by all members of a group 共享的；共有的
5. **Nigerian** /naiˈdʒiəriən/ *n.* 尼日利亚人
6. **Brazilian** /brəˈziliən/ *n.* 巴西人
7. **patron** /ˈpeitrən/ *n.* regular customer 顾客；主顾
8. **accordingly** /əˈkɔːdiŋli/ *ad.* in a way that is decided by something else 相应地；依照；根据
9. **adverse** /ˈædvəːs/ *adj.* bad or harmful 不利的；有害的
10. **aversion** /əˈvəːʃən/ *n.* strong dislike 反感；不喜欢
    to take/have an aversion to something 对……产生反感；厌恶
11. **physical** /ˈfizikəl/ **contact with** (*a phrase*) the state of bodily touching or communication 身体上(与人)接触
12. **conveyance** /kənˈveiəns/ *n.* vehicle 交通工具
13. **extensive** /iksˈtensiv/ *adj.* covering a wide area or a lot of things 广泛的；多方面的
14. **prolonged** /prəˈlɔŋd/ *adj.* for a length of time 长久的
15. **minimize** /ˈminimaiz/ *v.* to lessen something to the smallest possible amount or degree 使……减至最少；使……减至最低
16. **bump into** (*phrasal verb*) to strike or knock (someone, something) with force or violence 碰；撞
17. **inadvertently** /ˌinədˈvəːtəntli/ *ad.* without paying attention to or by accident 不经心地；疏忽地
18. **violate** /ˈvaiəleit/ *v.* to disagree or act against 背弃；违背
19. **notion** /ˈnəuʃən/ *n.* an idea; belief; opinion or concept 想法；见解；观念
20. **aggressive** /əˈgresiv/ *adj.* always ready to quarrel, fight or

Unit Two Manners and Courtesies

attack 爱挑衅的；咄咄逼人的

21. **sidewalk** /ˈsaidwɔːk/ *n.* a hard path by the side of a street 人行道

22. **hallway** /ˈhɔːlˌwei/ *n.* a narrow room that connects other rooms in a house or a building 走廊；过道

23. **stairways** /ˈstɛəweiz/ *n.* a set of steps to the up-floors 楼梯；走道

24. **progress** /ˈprəugres/ *v.* to develop; to improve or move forward over a period of time 发展；前进

25. **queue** /kjuː/ *v.* to form a line 排队

26. **registrar** /ˌredʒisˈtrɑː/ *n.* a person who is in charge of registering, a person who is on the list of registration 管登记（或注册）的人（尤指大学中主管学生注册的管理者）

27. **reflect** /riˈflekt/ *v.* to think about something that has happened 反省；反馈；深思

28. **privilege** /ˈprivilidʒ/ *n.* an advantage or right given to only one person or a group of people 特权；特别待遇

29. **jostle** /ˈdʒɔsl/ *v.* to push or shove 推；挤

30. **evoke** /iˈvəuk/ *v.* to call forth 引起；唤起

31. **hostile** /ˈhɔstail/ *adj.* against someone or something in a very angry or unfriendly way 敌对的；不友善的

32. **First come, first served.** (*a proverb*) 先来的先招待

33. **give priority to** (*a phrase*) to give attention, consideration, service etc. before or earlier than others 给……以优先权；（最）优先考虑

34. **stationary** /ˈsteiʃənəri/ *adj.* not moving 静止的；不可移动的

35. **inconsiderate** /ˌinkənˈsidərit/ *adj.* not caring about how your actions will affect people or upset them 考虑不周到的；不体谅的

36. **obstruct** /əbˈstrʌkt/ *v.* to block one's way or make it difficult for someone to do something 阻碍；妨碍

37. **deem** /diːm/ *v.* to think; to estimate 思考；估计

38. **parade** /pəˈreid/ *n.* a procession of people to celebrate a special day or event （庆祝）游行

39. **athletic** /æθˈletik/ *adj.* relating to sports 体育的；运动的
40. **contest** /ˈkɔntest/ *n.* a competition 竞赛；比赛
41. **interpret** /inˈtə:prit/ *v.*
    to understand 理解
    to repeat the words that a person speaks in another language 诠释；口译
42. **manifestation** /ˌmænifesˈteiʃən/ *n.* evidence; a public demonstration 表明；公开声明
43. **assumption** /əˈsʌmpʃən/ *n.* a belief that you think is very likely to be true 假定；设想
44. **as a rule** (*a phrase*) usually; generally 通常；一般来说
45. **farewell** /ˈfɛəˈwel/ *n.* good-by 再会；告别
46. **put out** (*phrasal verb*) to stop a fire, cigarette, etc. from burning 熄灭；扑灭
47. **anti-** /ˈænti-/ (*a prefix*) acting against or opposed to 反；抗；阻；排斥
48. **headway** /ˈhedwei/ *n.* progress; going forward 前进；进展
49. **outlaw** /ˈautlɔ:/ *v.* to make illegal; to declare (something) unlawful 宣布……为不合法；宣布在法律上失效
50. **designate** /ˈdezigneit/ *v.* to indicate 标明；标志
51. **prohibit** /prəˈhibit/ *v.* officially not to allow an activity or say that it is illegal 禁止
52. **formulate** /ˈfɔ:mjuleit/ *v.*
    to work out 制定
    to state systematically 用……公式表示
53. **specify** /ˈspesifai/ *v.* to mention or require something specially 详细说明；指定
54. **in the presence of** (*a phrase*) with someone being present 在眼前；在面前
55. **extinguish** /iksˈtiŋgwiʃ/ *v.* to put out or stop (a fire) 熄灭；扑灭
56. **discontinue** /ˈdiskənˈtinju/ *v.* to end or stop 中止；中断
57. **vigorous** /ˈvigərəs/ *adj.* active and energetic 朝气蓬勃的；精力充沛的

Unit Two Manners and Courtesies

58. **campaign** /kæmˈpein/ *n.* series of planned activities to gain a special result 运动；竞选运动
59. **aim at** (*phrasal verb*) to point at or direct to 对准；瞄准
60. **discourage** /disˈkʌridʒ/ *v.* to make someone feel less confident and hopeful 使……灰心；使……气馁
61. **take up** (*phrasal verb*) to start doing an activity 开始从事
62. **postpone** /ˌpəustˈpəun/ *v.* to delay till later 延迟；延期
63. **portion** /ˈpɔːʃən/ *n.* part of a whole; a share 一份，一部分
64. **sensitivity** /ˌsensiˈtivɪti/ *n.* the quality, state, or degree of being sensitive 敏感性；灵敏性
65. **offense** /əˈfens/ *n.* making someone displeased, angry or upset 得罪；冒犯
66. **light up** (*phrasal verb*)

    to start something burning 点燃

    to make something very bright 照亮
67. **confine** (**someone or something**) **to** (*phrasal verb*) to keep within bounds; to shut or lock up 限制在；锁入；关入
68. **accede** /ækˈsiːd/ *v.*

    to give in; to submit 妥协；顺从

    to agree to a request or suggestion, demand, etc. often unwillingly 不情愿地同意或答应

Content Questions

1. Why are foreigners constantly reminded that they are indeed foreigners?
2. What is people's behavior in public places subject to?
3. At what volume should a foreign visitor speak or talk in the U.S.?
4. Why is pushing one's way through a crowd considered quite rude in the U.S.?
5. What do Americans do whenever groups of people are walking in two opposite directions?

6. What does the notion "Line up, and wait your turn." reflect?
7. What is the definition of "First come, first served."?
8. How do you define the notion "Don't block the traffic."?
9. What is the interpretation of "Don't block the view."?
10. What should foreign smokers do before they start smoking?

A Question for Thinking and Discussion

How do Chinese differ from Americans in their behavior in public places?

4. Table Manners

There are many differences in table manners in different cultures. It is really worth your time to learn about how to behave while eating in other countries. Knowledge of table manners will show your international qualifications.

Don't make noises with your mouth. Close your mouth when eating. People make mouth noises because they eat without closing their mouths. When you drink your soup, don't sip it, but swallow it all in one mouthful.

Don't talk with your mouth full. If someone talks to you, wait until your mouth is empty before answering.

Imagine you are eating with

Unit Two Manners and Courtesies

someone you have just met. He spits bones onto the table. He wipes his mouth on his sleeve. He rushes for the best piece of food that is served. He does not have good table manners.

Fortunately, most of us eat neatly and are not greedy. These two points are the basic rules of good table manners.

Different cultures of the world have different table manners because of the food served, utensils used or not used and national customs. By knowing the table manners of different cultures, we show that we are willing to learn from them. That is a sure way to make friends.

There is not much call for a complete working knowledge of table manners in America today. Many families only gather all at once around the dinner table at holiday feasts, and most restaurants are too casual to require, or even to allow for, more than basic good

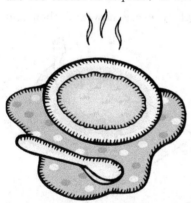

table manners. If, having dropped his napkin, a diner at a bistro were to attempt to practice proper etiquette by signaling a member of the staff to bring a fresh one, he would probably have to do without a napkin at all. Try as he might to make eye contact and indicate the nature of the problem with a subtle wiggle of the eyebrow and downward flicker of the glance, he is likely to succeed only in causing his date to think he is making a play for the server. Although strict good manners forbid placing a used eating utensil back on the table, the server removing a plate on which a fork has quite properly been positioned "pointing at 11 o'clock" might just plop that item back where it started, making more of a clatter than if the diner had simply done it himself/herself.

From time to time, perhaps at an important business dinner, a romantic date at an expensive restaurant, or a first dinner with the family of the person who may be "the One" —it is necessary to display a more sophisticated knowledge of table etiquette. This is not difficult, once you have mastered the basics. Anyone armed with this core knowledge and the ability to adapt smoothly to the situation at hand will be able to handle even the most formal event. The goal is not, after all, to demonstrate utter mastery of the most arcane details, of etiquette (which would be quite difficult considering the wide variations of customs in different cultures and from generation to generation), but rather to behave with graciousness and poise at the table.

Posture

Proper posture at the table is very important. Sit up straight, with your arms held near your body. You should neither lean on the back of the chair nor bend forward to place the elbows on the table. It is permissible to lean forward slightly every now and then and press the elbows very lightly against the edge of the table, if it is obvious that you are not using them for support.

Having Soup

Dip the spoon into the soup, moving it away from the body, until it is about two-thirds full, then sip the liquid (without  slurping) from the side of the spoon (without inserting the whole bowl of the spoon into the mouth). The theory behind this is that a diner who scoops the spoon toward himself is more likely to slosh soup onto his lap, although it is difficult to imagine what sort of eater would stroke the spoon so forcefully through the liquid that he creates waves. It is perfectly fine to tilt the bowl slightly—again away from the body—to get the last spoonful or two of soup.

Offering Food

Take note, when you are the host of a party, of the way you

offer additional servings to your guests. Urging someone to "have another (or a second or third) helping" can be seen as an unpleasant insinuation that the guest has eaten too much. It is best to phrase each offer of food as if the dish has just been brought out for the first time.

"Please pass me the salt (pepper)!" The proper response to this very simple request is to pick up both the salt and the pepper and to place them on the table within reach of the person next to you, who will do the same, and so on, until they reach the person who asked for them. They are not passed hand-to-hand, nor should anyone other than the original requester sprinkle her food when she has the shakers in her possession. The reason for this is that American etiquette is not about efficiency. Often, the most refined action is that which requires the greatest number of steps to carry it out (as in, for example, the zig-zag method of handling a fork and knife).

Manners of Eating

Eating manners are very important since it is repeated many times every day. It must be done properly whether eating alone, with family, or with friends. You should train yourself in proper eating manners, whether alone or with your family. It will then become a natural part of your behavior, and you will be at ease at the table.

There are certain table manners that are necessary. Eat what is in front of you. Close your mouth while eating to avoid unnecessary noises. Do not start eating ahead of the elders. If you are the elder, do not start eating before everyone is at the table.

It is preferred that eating should not be done in silence. It is good manners to talk during meals. Topics should be nice stories suitable for eating. At the end of the meal, if hands are to be washed, the elder should be asked to do first.

Do not express your disapproval or dislike of certain foods. Either eat it or pass it over quietly. If you like it you eat it. If you dislike it, you set it aside.

Do not put in your plate more than you can eat. Leftovers should not be thrown out and wasted. Do not forget the poor and the needy that do not have the portion you are throwing away.

Manners of Drinking

Drinking manners are no less important. Do not pour your drink down your throat in one gulp. Drink it in three sips.

Do not breathe out in your glass. This will irritate others and will smudge the glass or the cup. Do not drink directly from the jug or the container. Besides being unhealthy behavior, others who could be irritated may want to drink after you.

Avoid Excess

Modesty is the hallmark of the common people. Keep it if invited to a feast or if you are presented with food or drink. Do not be gluttonous devouring food as if you have not eaten for a long time, or as if you have not seen such excellent food before. Do not sample every dish on the table. People, even generous hosts disapprove of greedy eaters. Be reasonable and moderate in enjoying the generosity of your hosts.

Mechanics of Eating

Correctly, no one should start eating until everyone has been served. However, if some people are served before others, the unserved should turn to the served, and say "Don't wait; please start." The served do so, but pick slowly at their food so that the others will be able to catch up.

The set of silverware facing you at a classy dinner can be formidable, but the rule is simple: use it from the outside in. That is, you use the outside spoon for your soup, the middle one for

Unit Two Manners and Courtesies

dessert, and the inner one for your coffee. The truth is, though, that nobody will notice or care if you use the salad fork for your cake.

We eat nearly everything with a fork, which most right-handed people hold in the right hand. If something has to be cut up, you switch your knife to the right hand, do your cutting, (holding the item in place with the fork in the left hand), then lay down the knife (on the side of the plate), switch the fork back to the right hand, stab the bite-sized piece with the fork, and eat. Got it? There are those (English people in particular) who laugh at our way of eating, preferring the efficiency of keeping the fork in the left hand and the knife in the right.

Forks or Fingers?

You use the fork even when facing a number of foods that easily could be eaten with the fingers. Generally, if something could grease up your finger, don't touch it. The exception is fried chicken, which may be seized between both hands. Bread and some other foods such as raw vegetables, may be eaten with the fingers. With bread rolls, we break off and butter one small piece at a time. Never stick your hand or your fork into a serving dish.

When the knife is not in action, it is most pleasing to have the free hand resting on the lap, although few people will mind a forearm resting on the table. The eating arm should rise off the table when carrying food to the mouth; the mouth must not be lowered to meet the fork or the spoon. One leans forward slightly to avoid drips in one's lap. Elbows are properly kept off the table, at least until the plates are cleared. Silverware should not be waved around while one is talking.

Spoon-feeding

Foods too liquid to be eaten with a fork are eaten with a spoon, soup, ice cream, and dessert. It is bad form to drink from your soup bowl, which should not be lifted from the table. The soup spoon is slightly larger than 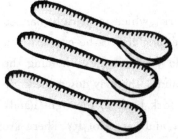 the dessert spoon, and you pour its contents into your mouth from its side, not from the tip. When you're finished, lay the spoon on the plate under the soup bowl. You're not supposed to leave the silverware in a sticking-up position. You show that you have finished by laying the knife and fork side by side on the right-hand side of the plate.

You should not burp, or slurp, at the table, although blowing one's nose is perfectly all right. Do not pick your teeth. Food should slide into your mouth as quietly as possible, then be eaten with the mouth closed. Most Americans hate the sight of the food in someone else's mouth. Therefore, you must swallow your food before speaking or at least have the appearance of having done so. Should someone suddenly ask if you realize that your wife is having an affair, you must still finish eating before replying.

Splitting the Check

My Chinese friend was amazed to hear of a father and two brothers who went out to dinner and split the check three ways. I assured him that in a family this is most unusual, but that among friends, splitting the check is common. Unless it was made very clear that someone else is paying, you are expected to pay your share of the check.

If you're with friends, and someone else grabs the check and says "Here, I'll get this", you might protest, but you can generally assume that the other person really means to pay.

A frequent question is whether to simply split the check in equal shares, or have each person pay for exactly what he/she ate. The person who says "Let's split it, shall we?" should not be the one who ate the most. This exactness horrifies many foreigners, but it

Unit Two Manners and Courtesies

means not so much stinginess on our part as our fondness for self-reliance and our idea of fairness. If you don't owe me and I don't owe you we have a nice even relationship.

● Words and Expressions

1. **qualification** /ˌkwɒlifiˈkeiʃən/ *n.* something that one achieves or learns that gives one the right and skills for something 资格；合格；证明

2. **sip** /sip/ *v.* to drink something gradually in small amount 呷；啜饮

3. **swallow** /ˈswɔləu/ *v.* to make something go down one's throat when eating and drinking 吞下；咽下

4. **spit** /spit/ *v.* to force a small amount of liquid, food, etc. out of one's mouth 吐；唾弃

5. **greedy** /ˈɡriːdi/ *adj.* filled with strong desire for more food, wealth, etc 贪婪；嘴馋

6. **utensil** /juːˈtensl/ *n.* a tool used for cooking, cleaning, or writing 器皿；用具

7. **feast** /fiːst/ *n.* a large meal on special occasion 盛宴；筵席

8. **napkin** /ˈnæpkin/ *n.* a piece of cloth or paper used when one is eating to keep one's mouth, hands and clothes clean 餐巾

9. **bistro** /ˈbistrəu/ *n.* a small restaurant, or a French café 小餐馆；小酒店

10. **etiquette** /ˈetiket/ *n.* conventions of social behavior 礼节；礼仪

11. **subtle** /ˈsʌtl/ *adj.* skillful; delicate 微妙的；难以捉摸的

12. **wiggle** /ˈwiɡl/ *n.* to move something side to side or up and down 扭动；摆动

13. **flicker** /ˈflikə/ *n.* unsteady movement 扑动；闪现

14. **plop** /plɒp/ *v.* to drop something with sound like that of object hitting water 啪的一声掉入；扑通一声落下

15. **clatter** /ˈklætə/ *n.* rattling sound 刀叉、碗碟等碰撞的铿锵声

16. **sophisticated** /səˈfistikeitid/ *adj.* complicated, complex; worldly-

wise 复杂的；老于世故的；有心计的

17. **master** /ˈmɑːstə/ *v.* to learn or do something well 掌握；使……精通

18. **core** /kɔː/ *n.* central part of something 核心；精髓

19. **adapt to** (*phrasal verb*) to be able or willing to change in order to be right in a new situation 使……适合；使……适应

20. **demonstrate** /ˈdemənstreit/ *v.* to show or prove something 证实；说明

21. **utter** /ˈʌtə/ *adj.* complete, absolute 完全的；彻底的

22. **arcane** /ɑːˈkein/ *adj.* known only to those with special knowledge 神秘的；秘密的

23. **graciousness** /ˈgreiʃəsnis/ *n.* kindness; politeness 谦和；礼貌

24. **poise** /pɔiz/ *n.* good judgment and self-control in one's action 沉着；坦然自若

25. **posture** /ˈpɔstʃə/ *n.* a particular position in which you stand, sit, etc.; post 姿态；姿势

26. **dip** /dip/ *v.* to put something into a liquid and take it out quickly again 浸；蘸

27. **slurp** /sləːp/ *v.* to eat or drink with loud sucking noises 啧啧地吃或喝

28. **scoop** /skuːp/ *v.* to move liquid by taking it up from or out of a container 舀起；铲起

29. **slosh** /slɔʃ/ *v.* to splash; to make water fly up when jumping in it or hitting it 溅；泼

30. **tilt** /tilt/ *v.* to (cause to) slope as by raising one end 倾斜；歪斜

31. **take note** (*a phrase*) to take notice of something or pay attention to something 注意到

32. **insinuation** /inˌsinjuˈeiʃən/ *n.* a hint given slyly; an indirect saying 暗讽；含沙射影

33. **phrase** /freiz/ *v.* to use a group of words to say or explain 用话表示；措词简洁

34. **response** /riˈspɔns/ *n.* an answer; an action done in answer 答复；反应

Unit Two Manners and Courtesies

35. **other than** (*a phrase*) except for 除了；非
36. **sprinkle** /'spriŋkl/ *v.* to scatter drops of a liquid or small pieces of something on something 撒；洒
37. **efficiency** /i'fiʃənsi/ *n.* state or quality of performing duties well 效率；效能
38. **refined** /ri'faind/ *adj.* being in good manners, tastes, etc. 文雅的；得体的
39. **zigzag** /'zigzæg/ *n.* a line or path which turns right and left alternately at sharp (equal or unequal) angles 之字形；Z字形
40. **be at ease** (*a phrase*) to feel relaxed and comfortable 自在；不拘束
41. **disapproval** /ˌdisə'pruːvəl/ *n.* unfavorable opinion 不赞成；非难
42. **leftovers** /'leftəuvəz/ *n.* food left after a meal 剩菜剩饭
43. **no less** (*a phrase*) 不少于；不亚于
44. **gulp** /gʌlp/ *n.* a large mouthful swallowing 吞咽；一大口
45. **smudge** /smʌdʒ/ *v.* to make something dirty 玷污；弄脏
46. **jug** /dʒʌg/ *n.* a container for liquids 有柄的大壶，大罐
47. **excess** /ik'ses/ *n.* something more than is reasonable 过量；过度
48. **modesty** /'mɔdisti/ *n.* the quality, state, or fact of being modest 节制；朴素
49. **hallmark** /'hɔːlmɑːk/ *n.* distinguishing characteristic 品质证明；特点
50. **gluttonous** /'glʌtənəs/ *adj.* greedy in eating 贪吃的；暴食暴饮的
51. **devour** /di'vauə/ *v.* to consume or eat something when one is very hungry 狼吞虎咽地吃
52. **sample** /'sɑːmpl/ *v.* to show nature or quality by a small amount of something 把……作为样品
53. **moderate** /'mɔdərit/ *adj.* not extreme; not large or small but just in between 有节制的；适度的
54. **the unserved** people who have not been served with food 未被布菜的人
55. **formidable** /'fɔːmidəbl/ *adj.* very impressive; fearful 令人生畏的；难对付的

56. **switch to**（*phrasal verb*）to shift, move from one position to another 变换；转换
57. **stab** /stæb/ *v.* to thrust or pierce with a pointed weapon 刺；戳
58. **bite-sized** *adj.* mouthful bite of (something) 一口大小的(食物)
59. **grease up**（*phrasal verb*）to put fat or oil on something 使……油污；使……油腻
60. **transfer** /træns'fəː/ *v.* to move from one place to another 转移；传递
61. **forearm** /'fɔːrɑːm/ *n.* arm between elbow and wrist 前臂
61. **sticking-up** *adj.* in a vertical position 竖立的
63. **burp** /bəːp/ *v.* to force gas out from one's stomach 打嗝
64. **slide into**（*phrasal verb*）to move easily or smoothly into 滑进；滑入
65. **split** /split/ *v.* to separate, divide, crack, burst 分开；劈开；裂开
66. **grab** /græb/ *v.* to seize eagerly 抓住；捏住
67. **protest** /prə'test/ *v.* to express objection 反对；抗议
68. **exactness** /ig'zæktnis/ *n.* precision, accuracy, strictness 确切性；苛刻
69. **horrify** /'hɔrifai/ *v.* to cause dread or intense fear to 使……恐惧，使……震惊
70. **stinginess** /'stinjinis/ *n.* the state of spending, using, or giving unwilling, miserly 吝啬；小气

Content Questions

1. What should you avoid doing at a formal (classy) dinner in the West?
2. What is a proper posture at a formal dinner?
3. How can a diner display a proper table etiquette?
4. What is a strict table etiquette when a person is taking soup?

Unit Two Manners and Courtesies

5. Why do you have to avoid excess at a dinner?
6. How does a host/hostess offer additional servings to the guests?
7. How do Americans respond to the request "Please pass me the salt (pepper)!"?
8. Why are eating manners very important in the West?
9. How do you use the set of silverware at a classy dinner?
10. Why do Americans prefer to split the check?

A Question for Thinking and Discussion

What is the contrast between Americans and Chinese at a dinner table?

5. Campus Social Relations

A "mixer" is a more-or-less public dance often held at the beginning of a semester by a fraternity, sorority, or some other campus group. Everyone is welcome, and people come for the purpose of making new acquaintances. It follows that, at a mixer, one should introduce oneself to other people and not hesitate to ask people of the opposite sex to dance.

Whereas a mixer is an open or public function, a party is a gathering for which an invitation (in writing or by word of mouth) is required. At some parties people are

expected to bring a date, while at others they come and meet.
Dating and Male-female Relations

In the United States, dates usually involve two people rather than a large group of people, although "double dates" (two couples) are common. There are, moreover, different kinds of dates. One is a "study date" or "coffee date" during an afternoon or evening on a week night, when two people go to study together in a library or get together to have coffee and talk. Another is an evening date on weekends (i. e. Friday and Saturday nights), when two people might go to a movie, concert, play, or party.

The majority of the foreign students attending colleges and universities in the United States are not married. In many cases, they are interested in finding companionship with members of the opposite sex. Since male foreign students in the United States far outnumber female foreign students, the former frequently turn their attentions to the United States women. This can lead to anxieties for both the male student and the woman, because neither can be quite certain of what sort of behavior is appropriate or expected. This may be partly because young people in the United States tend to mingle more freely with members of the opposite sex than do young, unmarried people in many other countries. They are usually taught, as they grow up, that it is good to have acquaintances with members of the opposite sex as well as of their own sex. Thus, by the time they reach high school age, most young people in the United States will be at ease in the company of members of the opposite sex.

Setting a dater or arranging to get together may be done several days in advance or agreed on spontaneously. The relationship between the two individuals concerned might be a casual acquaintance, a brother-sister type of friendship, an acquaintance with romantic overtones, a passionate involvement. While the two people planning to get together for a date may be contemplating marriage, it could also be true that they have no such intention at all and merely seek to enjoy each other's company. Whether or not a relationship between a particular male and female will culminate in sexual activity between them depends on their own feelings about each other and their own views or values about the propriety of sexual activity undertaken outside marriage.

When faced with this perplexing variety of possible attitudes, values, and practices, the recently arrived foreign student is likely to become confused. Indeed, it is not unusual for United States students themselves to become confused. As a result they may have trouble knowing how to become acquainted with a member of the opposite sex, how to find out what that person thinks or feels, what kind of relationships that person is looking for, and what kind of behavior that person expects in given situations. Obviously, in light of this, the foreign student will have to learn what opportunities for meeting others are available and how to find relationships that are satisfying for the student and whoever else is involved. To the end, here are some suggestions as to how students might get started:

When asking a woman for a date, the man should not ask the question "Are you busy Saturday night?" Instead, he should make a special proposal: "Would you like to go with me to a party at the International House Saturday night?"

The woman's reply is, of course, vital. She may say, "I'd like to, but I already have something to do Saturday. Maybe we could get together some other time." If she says that, the man should not be discouraged and should feel free to ask her again a week or two later.

If the woman simply say, "I already have something to do Saturday," and offers no suggestion about trying another time, it is probable that she means that she would rather not go out with the man. If the man has the impression that the woman does not want to go out with him, either because she gives a discouraging reply or repeatedly (twice) turns down invitations for dates, he should leave her alone. (What makes all of this difficult is that sometimes a woman does not want to go out with a man will not tell him so in a direct way because she thinks her candor might "hurt his feelings."

In such cases, the man should try to judge the woman's true feelings.)

When a man invites a woman for a date, he generally assumes responsibility for all expenses on the date. If the man continues to date the same woman, she may offer to pay part of the expenses. But it is assumed that the man will pay the expenses unless the woman offers to assist. A woman may also offer to cook dinner for a man as a way of "reimbursing" him for the money he has spent on previous dates with her. The man should, therefore, not feel hesitant about accepting such an invitation. If a group of people go out together, and no one has a special date, it is usually "Dutch treat," and everyone pays his or her own expenses.

If a man enjoys a date he has with a particular woman, and she indicates that she, too, has had an enjoyable time, he may ask her out again. If not, he can try again with someone else. Dating a variety of people does not indicate frivolity on the part of a man or promiscuity on the part of a woman.

It is important for a woman from another culture to remember that a young man from the United States may have different expectations of her than a man in her own society would have. She must therefore make clear to him from the start what her expectations are, and should make continuing efforts to understand his expectations. Only if their expectations are reasonable accord can a man and a woman expect to have a satisfying relationship.

Words and Expressions

1. **semester** /si'mestə/ *n.* either of the two periods into which a year at a schools and universities in the U.S. 学年中的一个学期
2. **fraternity** /frə'tɜːniti/ *n.* male society 〔美〕兄弟会；互助会
3. **sorority** /sə'rɔriti/ *n.* club of women and girls /〔美〕大学女生联谊会

Unit Two Manners and Courtesies

4. **whereas** /hwɛər'æz/ *conj.* showing an opposite; but; although 但是；可是；(表示相反的情况)而……；却……

5. **date** /deit/ *n. & v.*
   a person (of opposite sex) with whom one has a meeting 约会者；异性朋友
   to have a meeting with a person of the opposite sex 约会；与异性朋友会面

6. **majority** /mə'dʒɔriti/ *n.* the greater number or amount (esp. of people) 大多数

7. **companionship** /kəm'pænjənʃip/ *n.* the relationship of companions; friendly fellowship 伙伴关系；友好同伴

8. **outnumber** /aut'nʌmbə/ *v.* to be larger in number than 数量上超过

9. **mingle with** (*phrasal verb*) to mix with another thing or with people 混在一起；与……混合

10. **spontaneously** /spɔn'teiniəsli/ *ad.* unplannedly; produced from natural 自发地；自动地；未计划

11. **overtone** /'əuvətəun/ *n.* additional meaning; musical tone added to basic tone 额外的意思

12. **passionate** /'pæʃənit/ *adj.* showing or filled with strong, deep, often uncontrollable feeling, esp. of love, hatred, or anger 热情的；充满激情的

13. **contemplate** /'kɔntempleit/ *v.* to consider or look at something with continued attention 仔细考虑；沉思

14. **culminate** /'kʌlmineit/ *v.* to reach the highest point, degree, or development in 到达顶点(或高潮)；告终

15. **propriety** /prə'praiəti/ *n.* rightness of social or moral behavior 礼仪；礼节；规矩

16. **undertake** /ˌʌndə'teik/ *v.* to take up (a position); to start on (work) 担任；从事；进行

17. **perplexing** /pə'pleksiŋ/ *adj.* causing or feeling confused or troubled by being difficult to understand or answer 令人困惑的；令人难堪的

18. **in light of** (*a phrase*) taking into account; considering 鉴于;由于;根据

19. **proposal** /prəˈpəuzəl/ *n.* a plan or suggestion 提议;提案

20. **vital** /ˈvaitəl/ *adj.* very necessary; of the greatest importance 紧要的;至关重要的

21. **turn down** (*phrasal verb*) to refuse (a request or a person, etc.) 拒绝

22. **leave alone** (*phrasal verb*) to allow to be by oneself; to allow to remain untouched or unchanged 不加于干涉;让其独处;让它去

23. **merely** /ˈmiəli/ *ad.* only; to emphasize that something or someone is not serious, important, dangerous at all 仅仅;只不过

24. **candor** /ˈkændə/ *n.* the state of being sincerely honest and truthful 坦诚;直率

25. **reimburse** /ˌriːimˈbəːs/ *v.* to pay (money) back to (a spender) (正式)报销;报销费用

26. **hesitant** /ˈhezitənt/ *adj.* showing uncertainty or slowness about deciding to act; reluctant to do 犹豫的;踌躇的

27. **Dutch treat** to share expenses; to go Dutch with someone 各自付账

28. **frivolity** /friˈvɔliti/ *n.* the condition of being not serious; being silly 轻浮;愚蠢

29. **promiscuity** /ˌprɔmisˈkjuːiti/ *n.* the state of not being limited to one sexual partner (贬义)性方面乱搞;乱交

30. **accord** /əˈkɔːd/ *n.* to be willing to, want to 自觉;自愿

Content Questions

1. What is a "mixer" on campus?
2. What is the function of a "mixer" on campus?
3. What kinds of dates do people have on campus?

4. What may the relationship of the individuals of the opposite sex lead to?
5. What do you have to take note when you are going to date a member of the opposite sex on campus?
6. What does a man do if he wants to ask a woman for a date?
7. What should a man do if the woman gives a polite answer to his invitation or if the woman gives a discouraging reply or repeatedly turns down his invitations?
8. Who is usually responsible for the expenses on a date?
9. How do you define the notion "Dutch treat"?
10. What does dating a variety of people indicate in the U.S.?

A Question for Thinking and Discussion

Are there any similarities and differences between Chinese and American young people on a date? If there are differences, what are they?

Unit Three
LIFE STYLES AND PATTERNS

1. Pace of Life

Many visitors find the fast pace at which people move very troubling. One's first impression is likely to be that everyone is in a rush. City people always appear to be hurrying to get where they are  going and are impatient if they are delayed even for a brief moment. At first, this may seem unfriendly to you. Bus drivers will rush you; storekeepers will be in a hurry as they serve you; people will push past you as they walk along the street. You will miss smiles, brief conversations with people as you shop or dine away from home. Do not think that because Americans are in such a hurry that they are unfriendly. Often, life is much slower outside the big cities, as is true in other countries as well.

Americans who live in cities such as New York, Chicago, or Los Angeles, often think that everyone is equally in a hurry to get things done; they expect others to "push back," just as city people do in Tokyo, Beirut, or Sao Paulo. But when they discover that you are a stranger, most Americans become quite kindly and will take great care to help you. Those who first came to the city as strangers remember how frightening a new city can be. If you need help or want to ask a question, choose a friendly looking person and say, "I am a stranger here. Can you help me?"

Most people will stop, smile at you, and help you find your way or answer your questions. But you must let them know that you need help. Otherwise they are likely to pass you by, not noticing that you are new to the city and in need of help. Occasionally, you may find someone too busy or perhaps too rushed to give you aid. If this happens, do not be discouraged; just ask someone else. Most Americans enjoy helping a stranger.

Words and Expressions

1. **push back** (*phrasal verb*)
   to move something or someone further back 使……往后退
   to cause someone to move back 使……后移
2. **Beirut** /bei'ru:t/ *n.* 贝鲁特(黎巴嫩首都)
3. **Sao Paulo** 圣保罗(巴西一城市)

Content Questions

1. What sort of life do American city people lead?
2. What will you miss in the U.S. when everyone appears to be in a hurry?
3. What do most Americans do when they find that you are a stranger?
4. What would you do if you really need some help in a city of the U.S.?
5. What will be the responses of most American people if you ask for help?

A Question for Thinking and Discussion

Why do people in a modern city lead a fast pace of life?

2. Friendship Patterns

In any society where people frequently move from one place to another, friendships can be close and strong for a while and then disappear when the individuals move away from each other. Both individuals may write to each other for a year or two, then no more.

But if the same people meet again, even years later, they continue the friendship, and are delighted to associate with one another again. This can be confusing to people from countries where friendships develop more slowly but then become lifetime relationships, with each person trusting and feeling an obligation to the other, extending sometimes to both families.

Perhaps the most outstanding characteristic of the contemporary United States society is its diversity. It is therefore difficult, if not impossible, to make meaningful generalizations about it or even about special ethnic, religious, socioeconomic, age, occupational or other types of subgroups, since individual members of the society may belong to more than one of such groups at the same time or at different times.

Nevertheless, it is possible to mention certain characteristics that, in general, describe attitudes and practices that are common among the people of the United States. Following are some notable characteristics that may underlie or otherwise influence friendship patterns in the United Sates.

Individualism

People in the United States generally consider self-reliance and independence as ideal personal qualities. As a consequence, most people see themselves as separate individuals, not as representatives of a family, community, or other group. They dislike being dependent on other people or having others dependent on them. Visitors from other countries sometimes view this attitude as "selfishness." On the other hand, they may view it as a healthy freedom from the constraints of the ties to family, clan, or social class.

Informality

Many foreign students find that people in the United States are informal in dress, in decorum, and in personal relationships to a degree that seems at times extreme or, at best, inappropriate. The newly arrived foreign student should not be surprised if other students, teaching fellows, and even some professors use his or her first name and expect the student to call them by their first names, even after only a brief acquaintance. From the point of view of some people from other countries, this kind of informal behavior reflects a "lack of respect;" from the point of view of others, it reflects a healthy freedom from rigid social ritual.

Casual Friendship

The relationship between two individuals who regard each other as friends tends, in the United States, to be more casual than a comparable relationship between two people in many other cultures. Because they are taught to be self-reliant, because they live in a very mobile society, and for many other reasons as well, people in the United States tend to avoid deep involvements with other people. The result is sometimes viewed by foreigners as an "inability to be friends." Or it may be seen as normal way to retain personal happiness in a mobile, ever-changing society.

Time Consciousness

Considerable importance and value are placed on punctuality in the United States, and people in all walks of life tend to organize their activities by means of schedules. As a result, to the foreign observer they may seem hurried, always running from one thing to the next and not able to relax and enjoy themselves. Indeed, some visitors from other countries have concluded that United States society is "ruled by the clock." Others see this as a helpful way of assuring that things get done in an orderly fashion.

Materialism

"Success" in the United States society is often measured by the amount of money or quantity of material goods a person is able to accumulate. This is particularly true when the person has accumulated money and goods by means of such valued qualities as hard work, cleverness, and persistence. Some foreigners view this as a "lack of appreciation for the spiritual or human aspects of life," while others see it as a way of assuring the continuation of a comparatively high standard of living in the country.

Words and Expressions

1. **frequently** /ˈfriːkwəntli/ *ad.* happening often 时常发生;频繁地
2. **obligation** /ˌɔbliˈgeiʃən/ *n.* something that one must do 义务;责任
3. **extend** /iksˈtend/ *v.*
   to make something longer or larger 扩大
   to cover an area 扩展
4. **contemporary** /kənˈtempərəri/ *adj.* modern; of the present 当代的;现代的
5. **diversity** /daiˈvəːsiti/ *n.* difference; variety 多样性;多变化
6. **ethnic** /ˈeθnik/ *adj.* of or related to a racial; national; or tribal group 种族的;民族的
7. **underlie** /ˌʌndəˈlai/ *v.* (underlay, underlain)
   (of feelings and qualities) to form a (hidden) explanation of (指情绪和特性)成为……原因;成为……基础
8. **as a consequence** (*a phrase*) as a result; therefore 因此;所以
9. **constraint** /kənˈstreint/ *n.* something that limits one's freedom of action 约束力;自制力

Unit Three Life Styles and Patterns

10. **clan** /klæn/ *n.* (esp. in Scotland) a group of families; tribe 氏族;部落
11. **decorum** /di'kɔːrəm/ *n.* behavior that people consider to be polite and correct 礼节;礼仪
12. **inappropriate** /ˌinə'prəupriit/ *adj.* not right or suitable 不适合的;不恰当的
13. **rigid** /'ridʒid/ *adj.* stiff; not easy to bend 严格的;坚固的;固执的
14. **ritual** /'ritjuəl/ *n.* one or more ceremonies or customary acts often repeated in the same form 仪式;典礼
15. **consciousness** /'kɔnʃəsnis/ *n.* the condition of being able to think, feel, understand what is happening, etc. 知觉;意识
16. **punctuality** /ˌpʌŋktju'æliti/ *n.* being at the time fixed; being at the exact time 按时;准时
17. **accumulate** /ə'kjuːmjuleit/ *v.* to make or become greater in quantity and size; collect or grow into a mass 积累;积聚
18. **persistence** /pə'sistəns/ *n.* continuing in a habit, or course of action despite oppositions or warnings 毅力;持之以恒
19. **spiritual** /'spiritʃuəl/ *adj.* not of material things; of the nature of spirit or soul 心灵上的;精神上的

Content Questions

1. What is the most outstanding characteristic of the contemporary United States society?
2. What are the notable characteristics that may underlie or otherwise influence friendship patterns in the U.S.?
3. Why do American people see themselves as separate individuals?
4. How do American people display their informality?
5. Why do Americans have casual friendship?
6. How do you define "Time Consciousness"?
7. How is "success" measured in the U.S. society?
8. What is the foreigners' comment on the Americans' materialism?

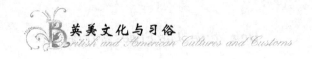

A Question for Thinking and Discussion

What is your comment on the American notable characteristics of Individualism and Materialism?

3. Housing

Prospective students should bear in mind that housing will be an expensive item in their budget, approaching in magnitude the cost of tuition and food. In general, the amount that a student spends for housing should be held to approximately one-fifth or one-fourth of the total available for living expenses (as opposed to educational expenses, such as tuition and fees). If the amount spent for housing reaches one-third of the total budget for living expenses, the student is certainly spending too much, however, if it drops to one-sixth, it is possible that the quarters are unsafe, unhealthy, and possibly illegal (if the landlord has failed to comply with local ordinances requiring that certain standards be maintained).

For detailed information on local housing alternatives, prospective students should contact the housing office and/or the foreign student adviser of the institution that has admitted them. Students should also be advised that commuting to campus from a distance is usually very difficult, because public transportation in many towns and cities in the United States is simply not adequate or convenient.

On arrival in the United States, students can usually obtain further information on local housing options from the foreign student adviser, the housing office of the institution, bulletin boards located

Unit Three Life Styles and Patterns

in dormitories, cafeterias, libraries, etc. on the campus, the "for rent" columns of campus or community newspapers, fellow students who attend the institution and a host family in the community. A local international hospitality organization may also be a source of assistance in finding a suitable place to live.

Types of Housing

Temporary Accommodations (On- and Off-campus)

If a student wishes to choose a place to live after arrival, or for some reason is unable to reserve in advance the dormitory room or university-operated apartment wanted, the student will need temporary lodgings while surveying the field and making arrangements to occupy more permanent quarters. On-campus, temporary lodgings are often available in dormitories. Such lodgings (guest rooms) may be rented on a per-day basis at very reasonable rates  (as low as $10—$15). Comparably inexpensive accommodations can usually be found in local YMCA/YWCA facilities or in the "International Houses" that are found in major cities. Hotels and motels, though often conveniently located in relation to the college or university campus, offer the most expensive temporary accommodations with rates as high as $35 to $45 per person, per day. Prospective students wishing to obtain further information concerning temporary lodgings should correspond with the foreign student adviser of the institution they plan to attend.

Often some advance arrangements can be made by or for the student to stay a few days with a fellow countryman. Also, newly arrived students are occasionally invited to be the house guest of a host family in the community until long-term living arrangements can be made. Obviously, for a married student whose family has accompanied him or her to the United States, it is likely to be more difficult and expensive to find temporary lodgings while a suitable

apartment is selected and rented.

Dormitories (Residence Halls)

  Many (but not all) United States colleges and universities own and operate student residence halls. When available, this housing typically consists of dormitories, apartment buildings, and occasionally a few separate houses for graduate students or married students and their families. Campus housing is generally the easiest type to reserve by correspondence from abroad and has the advantage of providing an assured living place that can be occupied immediately on arrival. On the other hand, it imposes the possible disadvantage of requiring that the student make an advance commitment without knowing exactly what is provided and what alternatives exist. The degree of disadvantage involved will depend on the accuracy and completeness of any brochures or information routinely mailed abroad to prospective foreign students.

  The residence halls found on United States campuses usually contain sleeping rooms as well as lounges and recreation areas, libraries and study rooms, dining rooms, snack kitchens, and laundry facilities. Graduate or senior undergraduate students are often employed as resident advisers, with responsibility for providing general assistance to their fellow residents, as well as establishing a student government for the dormitory, organizing an intramural sports program, and planning various social and recreational activities. In some instances, they also function as counselors on academic and personal problems. Except in university-owned international houses, graduates and undergraduates will normally be housed in separate buildings. Conventional dormitories or residence halls may be either restricted to one sex or coeducational, with certain floors or areas within them assigned to men or women. Undergraduate residence halls are made up of predominantly double rooms (with two separate beds) that combine sleeping and study areas (often equipped with individual desks and bookcases). Typically, the residents along a particular corridor on a floor of the building share one or more large bathrooms. Single rooms are usually available for the student who does not wish to share with another person. However, such rooms are more expensive.

Students wishing to live in a residence hall on campus must sign a contract or agreement to occupy such quarters for a specified period of time. Contracts are either for a full academic year (nine months) or for a semester or quarter and frequently stipulate that the student must pay for a certain number of meals in the hall dining room each week of the contract period. Hall dining room menus offer some choice of food, but may fail to satisfy some of the dietary preferences and obligations of foreign students who are non-Christians. Before signing a dormitory room and board contract, the student should read it carefully and ask for a clear explanation of any of its language that is not clear.

In recent years dormitories and other on-campus living accommodations have become less expensive, and therefore more popular, relative to off-campus housing alternatives. Indeed, on some campuses, the demand for dormitory rooms has exceeded the number of residential units available.

Apartments (On- and Off-campus)

Apartment units that are owned and operated by colleges are generally restricted to occupancy by married undergraduate or graduate students, graduate students only, or members of the institution's faculty and staff. As with privately owned off-campus apartments, some are unfurnished (except for a cooking stove and refrigerator) and thus may be unsuitable for the foreign couple whose budget does not allow for the purchase or rental of furniture. Furnished apartments are equipped with the essential bedroom, living room, and dining room furniture but do not include kitchen utensils, pots and pans (which may sometimes be obtained on loan from an active international hospitality organization on campus or in the community), or bedding (sheets, blankets) and towels which must be purchased. Apartments owned by colleges or universities may be reserved in advance, but the demand for them is often greater than the supply, making it necessary for the applicant to find temporary lodgings until a vacancy occurs. Monthly rents range from $275 to $375, depending on the size and variable supply-and-demand situation in different localities of the United States.

There is also a considerable range in the price and quality of privately owned apartments. Those located in old residences may be comparatively inexpensive, while the rents charged for newer, first-class, or luxury apartments may be well beyond the budget of many foreign students. Since the former are sometimes poorly maintained and hazardous to health and safety (with inadequate fire escapes, ventilation, and plumbing), the newly arrived foreign student should inspect an older apartment carefully before making any commitment to rent it. Also, if possible, the student should be accompanied by someone who is reasonably familiar with rental procedures (preferably a well-informed, long-time resident of the community) and can advise on the advantages and disadvantages of the particular apartment under consideration. At some institutions, this type of assistance is provided by volunteer community hospitality workers, by student groups, or by university housing officials. Often a foreign student (perhaps a fellow countryman) who has been on the scene a year or two can provide the new student with valuable assistance. The international student organizations at many institutions provide such assistance as part of their own welcoming programs for newcomers from abroad.

In general, in inquiring about an apartment it is advisable to ask about heating; utilities; furnishings; responsibilities for maintenance and repairs; rules about guests, pets, children; and so forth. If a written agreement (lease) is required, it should be read carefully and understood fully before being signed; once signed, it is a legally binding contract. Once again, the student should request an explanation of any language (especially legal terms) used in the lease that is not clear. Finally, if possible, students should avoid committing themselves to a long-term tenancy agreement (such as a one-year lease), since the initial selection of a place to live is seldom the best one. As they become more familiar with the campus community, and with the capacities and limitations of their budget, they may want to move to other quarters that offer greater advantages than the apartment currently occupied. However, it is not always easy to find an apartment with a lease of less than a year.

Student Fraternities, Sororities, and Clubs (*On- and Off-campus*)

At many colleges and universities, student housing is provided by fraternities, sororities, and various student clubs. In general, these are closely knit, private social organizations of students who share certain beliefs, have common interests, as well as more-or-less similar preferences for a particular life style, including various social, recreational, and athletic activities. Usually such organizations have from 40 to 60 members and own large houses that provide living, dining, and social accommodations. Membership in a fraternity, sorority, or other student club may be by invitation "rushing" only; however, some fraternities and sororities regularly provide living accommodations for eight students who are nonmembers. The cost of living (room and board) in a fraternity or sorority house compares favorably with that of living in a dormitory.

How to Begin Looking

As is true in cities everywhere in the world, the farther you live outside the city, generally the lower the rents will be. However, traveling to and from the city by bus, car, or train may make it as expensive as living in the city. Naturally, it is easier to join in the life of a city if one is close to the center and, for this reason, you may prefer to live as close to the center of the city as possible. Or, you may prefer to rent a place for only a month or two until you become more familiar with the area.

Your best source of information about either houses or apartments is likely to be the local newspaper. Usually, the week's most complete listing of houses or apartments to rent appears in the

Sunday newspaper, which, in many cities, can be obtained late Saturday night. Many people looking for houses or apartments believe that they have a better chance of finding a place to live if they have all the information as soon as possible. On Sunday morning, they are ready to call or visit.

If You Rent a House

In every city and town there are people known as real estate agents who will help you find a house to rent. But they may charge a fixed sum of money, such as a month's rent or a percentage of the year's rent, to help you find a place. Some companies pay the amounts for their workers; others do not. If you have a job in the United States, be certain that you ask if your company or superior will pay for this service before you sign any papers with a real estate agent. You can also find a house by yourself by noticing "For Rent" signs and following newspaper advertisements. The sign will list a telephone number for you to call.

When you rent a house, in addition to the rent, you will generally be expected to pay for what are called utilities—gas and electricity, heat and hot water—and for simple electrical and other repairs. However, it is a good idea to be sure exactly what the rent does and does not include. As is the case with most house rentals, you will probably be expected to have certain responsibilities for the care of the house, such as grass-cutting and snow-removal. For example, in most cities, you, not the city, are responsible for clearing the walk of snow in front of the house within a few hours after each snowfall.

Furnished Apartments and Houses

The word "furnished" means different things to different people. Normally, a furnished apartment or house will include kitchen furniture such as a stove and kitchen supplies, bed or beds, chairs, tables, lamps and sometimes, but not always, a small supply of sheets and blankets. You are expected to supply the rest. You certainly will want to have enough of your own things to make you

Unit Three Life Styles and Patterns

feel familiar and comfortable. Your own pictures and books will make the apartment or house seem more like "home" to you.

One more word of guidance: What will the climate be like in that part of the United States to which you are going? If you will be in sunny California on the West Coast, hot Arizona in the Southwest, or moist Florida on the Southeast Coast, you should consider leaving warm clothing at home.

What Do the Rental Words Mean?

Even Americans are confused by the words used in advertisements for apartments or houses. For example, sometimes kitchens and bathrooms are counted as rooms, and sometimes they are not. When you see "2/1 or 2 rooms" listed, you cannot be certain what this means. Neither can Americans. The only wise thing to do is to ask in each cases. "Exactly what rooms are included in this apartment?" Ask to see a floor plan if you can, ask the size of the rooms. On what floor is the apartment. Usually, apartments are more expensive on the higher floors, because there is less noise, a better view, and usually more light.

Rental Agreements

Do not sign any agreement or lease until you have studied it carefully or asked a lawyer or some other knowledgeable person to read it. A lease is a written agreement giving you the right to use the apartment or house for a certain length of time in exchange for rent. You should understand in advance what the lease says about: ending the lease; extending it if you want to stay longer; number of occupants; rules concerning children or pets; who is responsible for repairs or damages; and whether you are permitted to rent the place to someone else.

Rents are normally payable one month in advance, usually on the first day of each month. In addition, when you lease an apartment, you are usually asked for the amount of one month's rent to be kept by the owner. This money—called a security deposit will be returned to you when you leave if there has been no major damage to the apartment or house during your occupancy. It simply assures the owner or someone who represents him, that if you damage the apartment or house, money is available for repair. Therefore, you should examine the apartment carefully before you sign a lease. If you notice any damage, or section of the apartment in need of repair, ask the owner or his representative to agree in writing that the damages existed before you rented the place. If, for any reason, you do not think you will be able to rent the apartment for the entire time stated in the lease, you should discuss that possibility before you sign.

Briefly, these are questions to consider before you sign any rental agreement:

* Which services are or are not included in the rent (such as electricity, gas, heat, or washing machine)?
* If a company found the house or apartment for you, must you pay them for the service?
* Will the apartment be repainted? Who will pay for the repainting?
* How long is the lease?
* What are the conditions under which you can end the lease?
* Does the house or apartment allow children or pets?

Public Utilities

Public utilities are the water, gas, and electricity provided to the public. Stoves are heated either by electricity or natural gas. Some people prefer electric stoves because, although they are slower to heat, the heat is considered more even. Most buildings are heated by gas or oil burners. A majority of the modern apartment buildings also have a central air conditioning system for cooling, which can be controlled by the occupants of each apartment. If you live in an older building, it is likely to have air conditioning machines in the windows, if there are none, it is possible to rent one during the summer months.

If you rent a house, you will receive bills each month for the gas and electricity you used during that period. These bills are not included in the monthly rent. Most of the United States uses 110—120 electricity, 60 cycles. Before bringing any machines that operate electrically, check to determine if they can be used in the United States.

Local Transportation

Private automobiles remain the most common form of local transportation in the United States, although the situation may be changing significantly in the next few years as a result of the continuing energy crisis. The cost of operating an automobile has become prohibitive for some people in the United States, especially students and others with limited means.

Owning and operating an automobile in the United States is a serious responsibility, and students should consider carefully before deciding to learn to drive or to buy a car. People who own automobiles must have a valid license for driving in the state in which they reside, insurance (which is very expensive. —with premiums amounting to hundreds of dollars annually), and registration (the car must be registered by the state in which its owner lives). In addition, some states have a personal property tax that adds to both the initial price of the car and the cost of maintaining it each year.

International driver's licenses may be used temporarily to allow persons from other countries to drive their cars in the United States. But students who plan to remain in the United States for more than a few months should obtain a driver's license from the state in which they reside.

When purchasing a car, it is advisable for the foreign student to be accompanied by an American who is familiar with the procedures involved, price ranges, and so forth. In order to operate the car that the student has purchased, it will be necessary to purchase automobile insurance. There are a large number of insurance companies that sell such insurance, and a wide variety of automobile insurance policies and related services available to automobile owners in the United States.

Buses, Subways, Commuter Trains

The type and extent of rapid transit service available in a given town or city in the United States depends on the size (population, area), terrain, and wealth of a community. Bus, subway, and commuter train fares generally are higher than in other countries. In some cities, people who use buses or subways must purchase special coins or tokens before riding on these conveyances. In other cities, one must pay the exact fare to be allowed aboard.

Taxis

While taxis are available in most United States communities, the fares charged for short distance transportation are high in comparison with taxi fare rates in most other countries. In general, taxis that operate in larger towns and urban centers have meters. The rider must pay the amount shown on the meter and is expected to add a tip to the driver.

Words and Expressions

1. **prospective** /prəsˈpektiv/ *adj.* likely and potential 未来的；可能成为的
2. **bear (something) in mind** (*a phrase*) to keep something in mind 把……牢记在心
3. **budget** /ˈbʌdʒit/ *n.* a plan of how to spend money 预算；预算案
4. **magnitude** /ˈmægnitjuːd/ *n.* greatness of size or importance （数量上）巨大；（程度上）广大
5. **approximately** /əprɒksiˈmətli/ *ad.* nearly correct but not exact 大致上；大体上
6. **expense** /iksˈpens/ *n.* money that one spends on something 花费；支出
7. **as opposed to** (*a phrase*) as completely different from; in contrast to 与……相对；与……相反
8. **quarter** /ˈkwɔːtə/ *n.* a part of a town or a place for certain

Unit Three Life Styles and Patterns

people to live 居住区

9. **illegal** /iˈliːgəl/ *adj.* not allowed by the law or against rules and regulations 非法的；违规的

10. **comply with** (*phrasal verb*) to act in accordance as someone demands 照做

11. **ordinance** /ˈɔːdinəns/ *n.* law, rules, regulations 法令；条例

12. **commute** /kəˈmjuːt/ *v.* to travel between home and work 经常来往于

13. **adequate** /ˈædikwit/ *adj.* sufficient; fit 充分的；足够的；适当的

14. **option** /ˈɔpʃən/ *n.* a choice that one makes in a particular situation 选择；选项

15. **bulletin board** a board on a wall for putting up notices 公告栏

16. **temporary** /ˈtempərəri/ *adj.* not lasting long 暂时的

17. **accommodation** /əˌkɔməˈdeiʃən/ *n.* a place to live 膳宿；容纳

18. **reserve** /riˈzəːv/ *v.*
    to arrange for a restaurant, table, a seat or a hotel room, etc. 预定
    to keep something available for 留作专用

19. **lodging** /ˈlɔdʒiŋ/ *n.* temporary housing, a room 寄宿；住所

20. **survey** /səːˈvei/ *n.* a general view or examination of a place or condition 调查；观察

21. **permanent** /ˈpəːmənənt/ *adj.* lasting for a long time or for all time 永久的；持久的

22. **YMCA** Young Men's Christian Association 基督教男青年会

23. **YWCA** Young Women's Christian Association 基督教女青年会

24. **correspond with** (*phrasal verb*) (*formal*) to write letters to someone 与……相互通信

25. **accompany** /əˈkʌmpəni/ *v.* to go somewhere with someone 陪同；伴随

26. **correspondence** /ˌkɔrisˈpɔndəns/ *n.* (*formal*) letters that people write to each other 通信；信函

27. **impose...on** (*phrasal verb*)
    to set as an obligation 把……强加于

to bring something in without welcome 硬塞

28. **commitment** /kə'mitmənt/ *n.* an obligation one should have 约定;承诺

29. **alternative** /ɔːl'təːnətiv/ *n.* something else one can do or use in a situation 二者之一;可采用的方法之一

30. **accuracy** /'ækjurəsi/ *n.* exactness and correctness 精确;准确

31. **brochure** /'brəuʃuə/ *n.* a thin book that gives information, especially about something one wants to know and buy 小册子

32. **lounge** /laundʒ/ *n.* a comfort room for sitting in, as in a house, hotel, or inn 休息室;起居室

33. **recreation** /ˌrekri'eiʃn/ *n.* activities that one does for enjoyment 消遣;娱乐

34. **intramural** /ˌintrə'mjuərəl/ *adj.* within one's area （国家、城市、团体）范围之内的

35. **counselor** /'kaunsələ/ *n.* an adviser 顾问

36. **academic** /ˌækə'demik/ *adj.* relating to schools, colleges, or universities or the subjects that one studies in them 学术的;高等院校的

37. **conventional** /kən'venʃənl/ *adj.* ordinary, common 普通平凡的;习俗的;常规的

38. **restrict** /ris'trikt/ *v.* to limit something carefully to particular people, purposes, or activities 限制;约束

39. **coeducational** /ˌkəuedjuː'keiʃənəl/ *adj.* with the system of educating both boys and girls in the same school 男女同校（教育）的

40. **predominantly** /pri'dɔminəntli/ *ad.* mainly; mostly 主要地;最显著

41. **contract** /'kɔntrækt/ *n.* a written agreement between two people that says what each of them must do 合同;契约

42. **specify** /'spesifai/ *v.* to say exactly what one wants, what will happen 具体指定;明确指明

43. **stipulate** /'stipjuleit/ *v.* to require as condition 规定;约定

44. **dietary** /'daiətəri/ *n.* food that one has to eat （每日）规定的食物

Unit Three Life Styles and Patterns

45. **occupancy** /ˈɔkjupənsi/ *n.* (period of) living in a particular place or on a piece of land 占用;居住

46. **faculty and staff** all the teachers and workers in a university 教职员工

47. **purchase** /ˈpəːtʃəs/ *v.* to buy something 购买;购置

48. **applicant** /ˈæplikənt/ *n.* someone who asks for a job, or a permission to study at a school 申请人

49. **vacancy** /ˈveikənsi/ *n.* a room which is available to stay in 空房

50. **hazardous** /ˈhæzədəs/ *adj.* dangerous or risky 危险的;冒险的

51. **ventilation** /ˌventiˈleiʃən/ *n.* circulation of air 通风;空气流通

52. **plumbing** /ˈplʌmiŋ/ *n.* system of water pipes, etc. 管道系统

53. **inspect** /inˈspekt/ *v.* to look at something carefully to find if anything is wrong 检查;视察

54. **procedure** /prəˈsiːdʒə/ *n.* course of action 过程;步骤

55. **maintenance** /ˈmeintinəns/ *n.* keeping something in good order or in good condition 维修;维护

56. **lease** /liːs/ *n.* a contract allowing someone to use another person's property(a house, vehicle, equipment) 租契;租约

57. **tenancy** /ˈtenənsi/ *n.* the temporary possession or occupancy of a house or a room that belongs to another person （房屋的）租用;租赁

58. **initial** /iˈniʃəl/ *adj.* of or at beginning 最初的;开始的

59. **capacity** /kəˈpæsiti/ *n.* the amount that something or someone can hold or make 能量;容量

60. **knit** /nit/ *v.* to form a netlike relationship （由于共同的利益、婚姻关系）联合;精密结合

61. **athletic** /æθˈletik/ *adj.* of or concerning a person who practices physical exercises or games that need strength and speed 运动员的;运动的;体育的

62. **estate** /iˈsteit/ *n.* (a large) piece of land in the country, usu. with one large house on it, the whole of a person's property 不动产;房地产

63. **agent** /ˈeidʒənt/ *n.* a person who provides service for people,

companies, or organizations 代理人；代理商

64. **superior** /sjuːˈpɪərɪə/ n. someone who has higher rank or position 上级；长辈

65. **utility** /juːˈtɪlɪtɪ/ n. a paid service that provides you with water, gas, electricity, etc. （水、气、电等）设施服务

66. **rental** /ˈrentl/ n. an amount of money paid to rent a vehicle, a house, or a piece of equipment 租金；租费

67. **moist** /mɔɪst/ adj. slightly wet or humid 潮湿的

68. **occupant** /ˈɔkjupənt/ n. a person who lives in a house or take possession of something 占用人；居住者

69. **security** /sɪˈkjuərɪtɪ/ n. safety, with no danger or risk 安全

70. **deposit** /dɪˈpɔzɪt/ n. part of the cost of something that one pays before he starts renting something 押金；定金

71. **section** /ˈsekʃən/ n. a part of something 部分

72. **representative** /ˌrepriˈzentətɪv/ n. someone who has been chosen to speak or do something for a person or a group 代表

73. **majority** /məˈdʒɔrɪtɪ/ n. the largest part of a group of people or something 大部分；大多数

74. **prohibitive** /prəˈhɪbɪtɪv/ adj. forbidden by law 禁止的；抑制的

75. **valid** /ˈvælɪd/ adj. (legal) effective because of being made or done with correct formalities, (of contracts, etc) having force in law 有效的；正当的

76. **reside** /rɪˈzaɪd/ v. to live or dwell 居住；驻扎

77. **premium** /ˈpriːmɪəm/ n. periodic insurance payment 保险费

78. **amount to** (*phrasal verb*) to add up to; to be equal to 合计；总共达到

79. **registration** /ˌredʒɪsˈtreɪʃən/ n. registering 注册登记

80. **transit** /ˈtrænsɪt/ n. passage or conveyance 运输；运送

81. **terrain** /ˈtereɪn/ n. stretch of land, esp. with regard to its natural features 地域；地带

82. **commuter** /kəˈmjuːtə/ n. a person who travels from his home to work 经常往返两地的人

83. **token** /ˈtəukən/ n. metal disk used as ticket, etc. 代用币；代价券

Unit Three Life Styles and Patterns

84. **conveyance** /kən'veiəns/ *n.* vehicles that carry goods or people from one place to another 运输工具

Content Questions

1. How much does the cost of housing take up in a student's living expenses?
2. What will be a quarter like if it is much cheaper than usual?
3. Where can a foreign student gain the detailed information on local housing options?
4. What will be a better place for a foreign student to stay temporarily before finding a suitable and permanent residence?
5. How can a foreign student get a living place reserved on campus before arrival?
6. What does a foreign student have to do if he/she wishes to live in a dormitory or residence hall on campus?
7. Who are usually occupants of the apartment units owned and operated by colleges?
8. Why does a foreign student have to reserve an apartment in advance?
9. What does a foreign student have to do before signing a contract?
10. What is the common form of paying the rent of an apartment or a house?
11. Why does a student have to pay a deposit before he/she moves into a house?
12. What is another issue that a student has to consider when he/she is looking for a living place?

A Question for Thinking and Discussion

What would you do if you were going to rent an apartment or a house in the U.S.?

4. Finding a Rest Room

A newly arrived visitor to the United States was recently asked what has been the most difficult thing for him on his first day in America.

Without a moment's hesitation, he answered "Finding a public bathroom."

Some countries have public rest rooms that are plainly in view on city streets or in small buildings that are clearly marked. The United States does not. In America, public restrooms are located in gasoline stations (which are clean and free, although one may need to ask the attendant for a key), airports, and bus and railroad stations, restaurants, libraries, large stores, theaters, and all places where the public is welcome are provided with rest rooms. You can go into any hotel and ask for the "Ladies' Room" or "Men's Room," even if you are not a guest at the hotel.

Don't be confused by the name on the doors of rest rooms. Sometimes they are marked "Men" or "Women" or "Ladies" or "Dames" or simply "Rest Room." There may be a picture or some other sign on the door indicating whether it is a men's or a ladies' room. Restaurants especially follow this custom. Women's rooms are often called "powder rooms." The European terms "comfort station" or "W. C." are rarely used in the United States, but generally understood.

○ Finding a Rest Room

1. **hesitation** /ˌhezɪˈteɪʃən/ n. slow signs of uncertainty or unwillingness in speech or action 犹豫；踌躇
2. **gasoline** /ˈɡæsəliːn/ n. a liquid burned in the engines of vehicles, ships, and planes to make them work 汽油

Unit Three Life Styles and Patterns

3. **attendant** /əˈtendənt/ *n.* someone whose job is to provide service for people 服务员;侍者

Content Questions

1. What is the most difficult thing for a newly arrived visitor to the U.S.?
2. Where can a foreign visitor find a public rest room in the U.S.?
3. What may confuse a foreign visitor when he/she is looking for a rest room?
4. What terms are rarely used in the U.S. to indicate a rest room?

A Question for Thinking and Discussion

What is the main difference between Chinese and Americans in finding a rest room?

5. Driving

"You can always tell when a car is being driven by a foreign student," said a Midwestern chief of police. "You don't have to be able to see the driver. They just don't drive the same way we do."

Foreigners' driving is noticeable anywhere. Driving entails not just the mechanical manipulations of the car—starting the engine, shifting gears, steering—but customary styles of driving as well. Driving customs vary from place to place, so foreigners' driving is often different from that of the natives.

Driving customs in America differ from one part of the country to another. In Pittsburgh, for example, a driver waiting at a red traffic light and wanting to turn left will race across the intersection in front of the oncoming cars just as the light turns green. Denver drivers will not do that; instead, they will wait until the oncoming traffic has passed and then they will make the left turn.

While there are marked regional differences in American drivers' behavior, there are some commonalities that foreign visitors who drive in the States will want to know about. After giving some general information about cars and driving in the United States, we will consider traffic laws, attitudes toward driving, and driving aids.

General Information

The ratio of motor vehicles to people in the United States is the highest in the world. Public transportation is generally not as accessible as it is in many other countries, and Americans tend to be too independent-minded to use common carriers anyway, so there are large numbers of cars. In 1985, 70,237,000 motor vehicles were licensed to operate in the United States. In many states the number of registered vehicles exceeded the number of licensed drivers.

Most Americans who have reached the age at which they can legally drive (the age is 16 in most states) have a driver's license. Females are as likely to drive as males.

Automobile accidents are not the grave social problem they are in some other countries, but they are still considered serious. In 1982 the rate at which fatal auto accidents occurred was 2.9 per 100 million vehicle miles driven, the lowest rate among countries for which data were available. By comparison, the rate was 3.4 in Finland and the United Kingdom, 4.8 in Japan, and 10.2 in Spain. A significant percentage of U.S. auto accidents involves drivers who have consumed enough alcohol to impair their judgment and reflexes. "Drunk driving" is considered a serious highway safety problem.

Unit Three Life Styles and Patterns

The U. S. road system is quite complex. State, county, and municipal authorities have responsibility for building, maintaining, and patrolling [with police] different highways and roads. Traffic laws vary somewhat from one jurisdiction to another, but there is general uniformity with respect to road signs, traffic lights, and the basic aspects of traffic engineering. (Some road signs are uniquely American; international signs are slowly being introduced.) Highways are kept as straight as possible. Except in the old cities on the East Coast, streets are generally laid out in a grid pattern unless geographical features make it difficult or impossible to adhere to that arrangement. Systems for naming and numbering streets vary.

Traffic Laws

Generally, American traffic laws cover the same subjects that traffic laws elsewhere cover: who can legally drive, minimum and maximum speeds, turning, parking, entering moving traffic, responding to emergency vehicles, vehicle maintenance, and so on. Drivers' licenses are issued by the separate states, usually through offices housed in county government buildings.

Traffic laws are enforced by state police on some roads, county sheriff's officers on others, and municipal police on still others. Police devote a significant portion of their time and effort to enforcing traffic laws. They issue what are called "traffic tickets," or simply "tickets," to violators. Drivers who get tickets normally have to pay a fine. In addition, most states have a "point system" whereby drivers are given points for each traffic offense. Drivers who accumulate a specified number of points will lose their driving privileges for a certain period of time. Serious or repeated traffic violations can result in incarceration.

Trucks, motorcycles, and bicycles—all of which are wheeled vehicles that use the roads are subject to traffic laws just as automobiles are.

Attitudes towards Driving and Traffic Laws

Drivers' attitudes probably explain more of their behavior on the road than do the traffic laws. Foreigners driving in the U. S. of course need to know what the traffic laws say, but they will also want to understand the ideas that govern American drivers' behavior.

Generally, Americans expect traffic laws to be enforced. They operate on the assumption that, at any time, a police officer might apprehend them if they violate the law. In general, American drivers take traffic laws seriously. A Southeast Asian high school teacher, in the States for advanced studies, learned how seriously when he tried to get an American driver's license. He failed the driving test twice before finally passing it. "They're so picky," he said of the driver's license examiners. "They kept saying I was breaking the laws." He had not stopped at some stop signs or given the required signals to indicate his intention to turn. In his own country such failures were quite acceptable.

Attitudes toward Other Drivers

Except for those—and there are many who are looked down upon for being "aggressive" or "discourteous," American drivers tend to cooperate with each other. They are not likely to be constantly competing to see who can get the farthest the fastest. If they see another driver trying to enter the flow of traffic, for example, they are likely to move over (if there is a lane for doing so) or even slow down or stop (if they are not going too fast) to allow the other driver to enter. If they see that another driver wishes to change lanes in front of them, they are likely to allow it.

The ideal is the "courteous driver," who pays attention to other drivers and cooperates with them in what is conceived as a joint effort to keep the roads safe for everyone. Like other ideals, this one is violated. But it is the ideal nonetheless.

At the same time there is constant awareness of the concept of "right-of-way." The traffic laws try to make clear which driver has the right-of-way in each possible driving situation. For example, drivers going straight have the right-of-way over those heading in the opposite direction and wishing to turn left. Drivers without the right-of-way are expected to yield to those who have it.

Attitudes toward Driving Safety

Americans generally assume that individual drivers are responsible for their own safety and that of other drivers around them. Traffic accidents are usually considered to result from carelessness or mechanical failure, and not from "fate," "God's will," or other forces beyond human control. But "accidents do happen," the Americans will say, referring to the fact that an accident can occur through a random configuration of circumstances or as a result of factors that drivers could not reasonably be expected to foresee.

Attitudes toward Pedestrians

Drivers' attitudes toward pedestrians vary from place to place. In some localities pedestrians are viewed as competitors for space on the roadway, and the burden is on the pedestrians to be wary. In other localities pedestrians are viewed as people whose wishes and apparent intentions deserve as much respect as those of other drivers.

One need only stand at an intersection and observe for a few minutes to see how local drivers and pedestrians view each other.

Words and Expressions

1. **entail** /in'teil/ *v.* to make (an event or action) necessary 需要；使……成为必要
2. **mechanical** /mi'kænikəl/ *adj.* relating to a machine 与……机械相关的；机械的
3. **manipulation** /mə'nipju'leiʃən/ *n.* skillful handling or controlling of something 操作；操纵
4. **shift** /ʃift/ *v.* to change position or move about 转换；转变
5. **gear** /giə/ *n.* the machinery in a vehicle that connects the engine to the wheels which makes them move (汽车)排挡
6. **steer** /stiə/ *v.* to make a vehicle, boat, or plane go in a

particular direction 驾驶;掌舵

7. **intersection** /ˌɪntəˈsekʃən/ *n.* place where roads meet 交叉点;十字路口

8. **commonality** /ˌkɔməˈnæliti/ *n.* common feature or attitude that is shared by two or more people 公共;普通

9. **ratio** /ˈreiʃiəu/ *n.* relative number or extent, proportion 比;比率

10. **accessible** /əkˈsesəbl/ *adj.* easy to get or get into 可得到的;可进入的

11. **grave** /greiv/ *adj.* serious or important 严重的,重大的

12. **impair** /imˈpɛə/ *v.* to damage or weaken 削弱;减少

13. **reflex** /ˈriːfleks/ *n.* automatic action or movement without thinking, as a habit or as a reaction to something 反映;反射

14. **municipal** /mjuːˈnisipəl/ *adj.* of a city 市政的,市立的

15. **patrol** /pəˈtrəul/ *v.* to pass through or go around in guarding 巡逻;巡查

16. **jurisdiction** /ˌdʒuərisˈdikʃən/ *n.* range of control; authority 管辖范围;权限

17. **uniformity** /ˌjuːniˈfɔːmiti/ *n.* condition of being the same throughout 一样;一致性

18. **uniquely** /juːˈniːkli/ *ad.* most unusually or rarely 唯一地;独一无二地

19. **grid** /grid/ *n.* covering of crossed bars; system of crossed lines 格子;格栅

20. **adhere to** (*phrasal verb*) to stick or cling to; be faithful or loyal to 坚持;依附;追随

21. **minimum** /ˈminiməm/ *n.* least possible quantity, degree, etc. 最小;最低

22. **maximum** /ˈmæksiməm/ *n.* greatest possible degree, quantity, etc. 最大;最高

23. **issue** /ˈiʃuː/ *v.* to send out; to distribute 分发;配给

24. **enforce** /inˈfɔːs/ *v.* to compel obedience to 实施;执行

25. **sheriff** /ˈʃerif/ *n.* country law-enforcement officer 县的行政司法

Unit Three Life Styles and Patterns

长官

26. **violator** /ˈvaiəleitə/ *n.* a person who breaks rules or regulations 违规者；违犯者

27. **accumulate** /əˈkjuːmjuleit/ *v.* to gather, collect, heap up 积累；积聚

28. **violation** /ˌvaiəˈleiʃən/ *n.* action of breaking rules or regulations 违反规定；违背条例

29. **incarceration** /inˌkɑːsəˈreiʃən/ *n.* being imprisoned, or being put in a jail 监禁；禁闭

30. **be subject to** (*a phrase*) to be liable to undergo 使……受到；使……遭遇

31. **apprehend** /ˌæpriˈhend/ *v.* to take into custody, arrest 拘留；逮捕

32. **picky** /ˈpiki/ *adj.* fault-finding, extremely fussy about something 好挑剔的；吹毛求疵的

33. **discourteous** /disˈkəːtiəs/ *adj.* impolite, lack of good manners 失礼；不礼貌

34. **conceive** /kənˈsiːv/ *v.* to form a plan or idea 构想出；想象

35. **joint** /dʒɔint/ *adj.* common shared or owned, done by two or more people 共同的；共有的

36. **nonetheless** /ˌnʌnðəˈles/ *ad.* in spite of what has been said, nevertheless 然而

37. **right-of-way** *n.* right of one vehicle to proceed before another 车辆等在公路上的优先行驶权

38. **yield to** (*phrasal verb*) to give way to; surrender 让位于；给予

39. **random** /ˈrændəm/ *adj.* occurring or done without aim or pattern 任意的；随意的

40. **configuration** /kənˌfigjuˈreiʃən/ *n.* external form 构造；形状

41. **foresee** /fɔːˈsiː/ *v.* to see beforehand, predict 预见；预知

42. **pedestrian** /peˈdestriən/ *n.* walker, someone who is walking rather than driving a car or riding a bike 行人；步行者

43. **wary** /ˈwɛəri/ *adj.* careful or cautious 谨慎的；小心翼翼的

44. **apparent** /əˈpærənt/ *adj.* clear and obvious 明显的；显而易见的

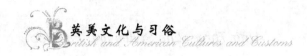

45. **deserve** /dɪˈzɜːv/ v. to be worthy of; be fit for 值得；应受

Content Questions

1. What does driving entail in the United States?
2. What does a foreigner have to consider if he/she drives in the U.S.?
3. Why is the ratio of motor vehicles of the U.S. the highest in the world?
4. What is considered a serious highway safety problem in the U.S.?
5. What do American traffic laws generally cover?
6. How do the States police enforce traffic laws?
7. What are American people's attitudes toward traffic laws?
8. What does a "courteous driver" usually do while driving on road?
9. What attitudes do American people have toward driving safety?
10. What are the American drivers' attitudes toward pedestrians?

A Question for Thinking and Discussion

How do Chinese drivers differ from those of the U.S. in their attitudes toward the traffic laws, other drivers, driving safety and pedestrians?

6. The Americans Living in the Suburban Houses

Since the 1960s, a lot of houses have been built in the suburbs, far from the centers of large cities. While more people are working in

Unit Three Life Styles and Patterns

and around big cities, most prefer not to live in city conditions.

As the suburbs grow, so the city centers tend to become mainly places for business. And except in the biggest cities which are tourist attractions in themselves, the central areas are losing commerce to the suburbs. In suburban areas shopping centers are being established, each  having a group of perhaps fifty shops around a huge car park; and the main unit of the shopping center is usually the supermarket. Modern American women are accustomed to buying all their food in weekly visits to the supermarket, bringing it home in the car and storing it in the deep-freeze.

Once an American has reached his home he is interested in working to improve it—making things, mending things, and work on the car—to make it as pleasant as possible. There is a strong desire to spend much free time at home when the home is well-equipped, comfortable and attractive; even the private swimming pool is no longer reserved for the very rich.

Americans invite their friends to their homes more than most people in Europe. Parties for children and for grown-ups are constantly occupying the leisure hours, usually with something to drink. In their suburbs Americans are extremely friendly and hospitable. They are also very interested in each other, and when a new family moves into a suburban house the neighbors will be calling at once to see if they can help in any way. The problem of personal social barriers has been overcome very much more successfully than in any part of Europe. The new suburb recreates the sense of community of the old country village. In it, a family's home is not an isolated island, but a part of a group of homes. Moreover, most find their homes more satisfying because they still have plenty of contacts outside the rural neighborhood. Most go to work in another place, so that the suburban home is only a part of their environment.

But Americans are a restless people who are always ready to move. So although they enjoy the life in the suburbs, they will by no means end their pursuit there. When his income rises as his career makes progress, he soon looks for a better house, in a better district, with more land, a better view, a bigger and finer swimming pool. He may be attached to the house which is home for the time being but this does not mean that he will put his roots there. Today's job, today's friends and neighborhood: all these are part of an American's identity. Instant coffee, instant friends—but nothing is seen as permanent. An American hopes and expects to exchange them all for something better; and he finds no difficulty in identifying himself with the new.

Words and Expressions

1. **suburban** /sə'bə:bən/ *adj.* of an area just outside a city where a lot of people live 郊外的
2. **commerce** /'kɔmə:s/ *n.* the business of buying and selling something 商业；贸易
3. **deep-freeze** /di:p-fri:z/ *n.* a piece of equipment used for keeping food frozen 冷冻冰箱
4. **constantly** /'kɔnstəntli/ *ad.* unchangingly or uninterruptedly 永恒地；不变地
5. **barrier** /'bæriə/ *n.* obstacle, obstruction 阻碍；障碍
6. **recreate** /'ri:kri'eit/ *v.* to create something new 再创造；重新创建
7. **isolated** /'aisəleitid/ *adj.* being kept alone, or being far away from 孤立的；隔离的
8. **pursuit** /pə'sju:t/ *n.* the act of seeking something as an aim or purpose 追求；寻求
9. **for the time being** (*a phrase*) for a limited period 暂时；眼下
10. **identity** /ai'dentiti/ *n.* who or what a particular person or thing

Unit Three Life Styles and Patterns

is 特性；个性

11. **instant** /ˈinstənt/ *adj.*
    happening immediately 即刻的
    food or drinks made quickly 即食的；即溶的

12. **identify** /aiˈdentifai/ *v.* to recognize or say who someone is or what something is 识别；验明；鉴定

Content Questions

1. What changes have taken place in the U.S. since 1960s?
2. What does an American do once he has reached home?
3. What constantly occupy American people's private hours?
4. What does the American new suburb recreate?
5. Why are Americans always ready to move?

A Question for Thinking and Discussion

Why do American people prefer living in the suburb to living in a city?

7. Leisure and Private Life in Britain

Life in modern Britain is probably following American trends with the collective activities of the family made easier by the motorcar and the house with its own garden. But the British still have their own ways to spend leisure and private hours.

In the past years night clubs have spread from London to other towns. Innumerable clubs and societies arrange dances and balls as social occasions for their members. People tend to get to such dances, in groups, having first had dinner together out or in the house of one of them. Dining out in a restaurant in the evening is not often in the province, though becoming less rare as the life improves. When they dine out, they look for restaurants which have exotic and unusual menus; There are a surprising number of them, some in quite small villages. Their good reputation attracts customers from far and wide.

A special British institution is the fish and chip shop, where it is possible to buy over the counter a piece of fried fish and potatoes. You can eat the fish and chips in the street as you walk along, or take it home if you live near by, and eat it on a plate. Most fish and chip shops close before 11 p.m., staying open late enough to serve people as they come out of cinemas. Snack bars and "espresso" coffee bars have great success among young people below the age for going to pubs.

Everywhere there are plenty of pubs, in which people play darts, talk and drink, usually while standing up. Every pub has its name, its sign and its "regulars," its customers who turn up night after night. A few old pubs have real character but many are dull and ugly. It seems that the English think it rather indecent for people to drink alcoholic drinks in any place where they can be seen from outside. So pubs usually not only have no tables outside, but are so built that it is impossible for people outside to see in, or for those who are inside to see out. There are exceptions to this, but not many. Pubs are meeting places for working men after the evening meal. With pint glasses filled with beer—in Scotland the national drink is whisky—they argue about football, the races, women. The traditional pub was a place for the men only. But things have changed, and more and more pubs are now places where men and women sit at tables, and they often provide good lunches. Most of them have a public bar, where drinks are slightly cheaper, and a saloon bar, which middle-class people usually prefer because it is

Unit Three Life Styles and Patterns

more comfortable and less crowded.

The teashop is almost as British as the pub. From 3:00 to 5:30 p.m., teashops offer you, as well as a pot of tea, bread and butter, scones, toast and jam, and cakes of varying quality. The Americans do not have afternoon tea, nor do they use teapots, which they consider old-fashioned. They are quite satisfied with teabags and a pot of hot rather than boiling water. The British say the American tea is like dish-water.

Among the middle classes, people who have children often fill their houses with children's parties, at which games are organized for twenty or thirty children before and after the Tea. Actually during the so-called Tea, there is no tea to drink, only fruit drinks, sandwiches, ice-cream and innumerable cakes. Although the well-to-do families may hurry their children off to boarding-schools at the age of eight, most modern parents take much trouble to give their children a good time while they are at home. Nurses have now disappeared, along with other servants, from the homes of all but the very rich. However, many mothers have au pair girls, usually from European countries and anxious to improve their English, to live with the family and help to look after the children. The strong impression that these girls have is that English children are spoiled.

Words and Expressions

1. **leisure** /ˈleʒə/ *n.* time when one is free from work or study 空闲；闲暇
2. **collective** /kəˈlektiv/ *adj.* doing or working by a group 集体的；聚合的
3. **trend** /trend/ *n.* tendency, increasing popular fashion or taste 趋向；倾向
4. **innumerable** /iˈnjuːmərəbl/ *adj.* very numerous, that cannot be counted 无数的；数不清的
5. **exotic** /igˈzɔtik/ *adj.* foreign, alien 外来的；外国产的

6. **reputation** /ˌrepjuˈteiʃən/ *n.* good name or public estimation 名誉；声望
7. **institution** /ˌinstiˈtjuːʃən/ *n.* organization with public purpose 公共机构；所址
8. **fish and chips** (*a popular English fast food*) *n.* fried fish and potatoes 油炸鱼和炸土豆条
9. **espresso** /ˈespresəu/ *n.* a strong coffee made with steam 〔意〕（用蒸汽加压）煮出的咖啡
10. **dart** /dɑːt/ *n.* game of throwing slender pointed missile at target 投镖游戏
11. **regular** /ˈregjulə/ *n.* something recurring at fixed time 固定节目、饮料等
12. **turn up** (*phrasal verb*) to arrive, to make one's appearance 抵达；发现；出现
13. **indecent** /inˈdiːsnt/ *adj.* not adequate; rough 不合适的；粗鄙的
14. **pint** /paint/ *n.* liquid or dry measure equal to one-half quart 品脱
15. **race** /reis/ *n.* group of people of common origin 人种；种族
16. **saloon** /səˈluːn/ *n.* public room 沙龙；交谊室
17. **scone** /skɔn/ *n.* small flat cake 烤饼
18. **well-to-do** /ˌweltuˈduː/ *adj.* rich or wealthy 富有的；宽裕的
19. **au pair** /əu pɛə/ *n.* a person, usually young foreign visitor or woman who does household tasks in exchange for room and board 〔法〕不取报酬，但是吃住在雇主家的女工
20. **spoiled** /spɔild/ *adj.* (esp. a child) selfish because of having too much attention or praise 溺爱的；宠坏的

Unit Three Life Styles and Patterns

Content Questions

1. What is the life like in modern Britain?
2. Where do the British go to spend their private hours?
3. Why do the British often visit the fish-and-chip shop?
4. Why are pubs so popular in Great Britain?
5. Why do middle class people prefer saloon bars?
6. Which place is as British as pubs in Great Britain?
7. What do middle class people often hold at home and why do they do so?
8. Who usually looks after the children of the well-to-do families?

A Question for Thinking and Discussion

How do you usually spend your leisure or private hours?

Unit Four
FOOD CUSTOMS AND EATING

1. Food Customs

Hotels

Most people start their visit to the United States by staying in a hotel. Like most countries, hotel restaurants are nearly always more expensive than neighborhood restaurants. In addition, hotel food is often not especially good and hotel dining rooms are sometimes dull. You might find it more interesting to wander along the nearby streets to see if you can find a place to eat that is less expensive and more fun. The words "coffee shop" in a hotel or airport indicate that prices are less cheaper than in a restaurant. Coffee shops offer a variety of light meals. "Snack bars" are sometimes cheaper than coffee shops, but they may be busier, requiring you to stand and eat at a counter.

Restaurants

Since America is a "melting pot," consisting of so many different nationalities, almost any kind of restaurant can be found in most of the large cities in America. And there is a great variety in the price in these restaurants. Restaurants invite people in various ways. Many restaurants put their menus in the window for the customer to know the price and the kind of food before coming in. But some

Unit Four Food Customs and Eating

restaurants do not post their menus, and if such a case occurs the customer can ask to see a menu before being seated at a table, or just ask about the price range. Never judge by appearance, which may be misleading. Those that look small and informal may really be very expensive; and those that look large and expensive may just be ordinary. In most city restaurants you are expected to pay $6—$8 a person for lunch and $10—$15 a person for dinner, with alcoholic drinks and wine extra. Prices are even higher in New York City.

Diners, looking like railroad cars, are found on campuses and on the outskirts of towns. The restaurants on campuses and on the outskirts of towns are very convenient to students, truck drivers and motorists by serving large portions of good, filling food at low prices. Another kind of eating place in America is drive-ins which are surrounded by parking lots, located just off a busy road. Traveling families or people who do not like to eat at their homes can drive in, park, order and eat. They may order food without even leaving their cars.

Reservations

If you are going to a restaurant for dinner, it is usually a good idea to telephone for a reservation. Cities are crowded and good restaurants will not hold reservations for more than a short time. If you cannot get into a restaurant because you have not reserved ahead, don't be angry. This frequently happens to Americans and visitors alike. Restaurants can only serve a certain number of people at one time, and if they are already filled, they must turn away any additional people who want to dine there. Frequently, a table will be available if you are willing to wait 20 or 30 minutes for it.

Bars

Bars are places where people gather to drink and enjoy themselves. In the United States, you will also see the words "cocktail lounge." Usually American bars and cocktail lounges are darker than those in other countries. In these bars, alcoholic drinks such as whiskey are served by the glass and beer is served by the glass or by the bottle. U. S. whiskey tends to be sweeter and cheaper than the whiskey of Scotland or Ireland. And the main U. S. whiskeys are made of corn or the blend of several grains called "blended whiskey." American beer is usually light and served very cold, and is very popular. According to the statistics, in one day, the Americans drink 90 million pounds of beer. European beers are available, too. Japanese beer is seen in the main cities. If you like to have your drink at room temperature, just say "no ice" to the waiter. Americans like most of their drinks cold with ice, including beer and Coke.

Informal Eating

Every country in the world has a variety of informal eating places where a person can get a quick, inexpensive meal. We have already mentioned snack bars and coffee shops. In the United States, there are also self-service "cafeterias." In a cafeteria, you walk through a line selecting your meal as you go along. They are very popular with Americans especially during the lunch hour. Although these "fast food" places are usually crowded with people at normal meal times (breakfast: 7:30 — 9:00A. M. ; lunch: 12:00 noon — 2:00 P. M. ; and dinner:6:00—8:00 P. M.), you can usually get a seat without waiting too long if you go a little before or after the usual meal-hour. Such places can be found everywhere and usually open long hours. You will find them useful in helping you save money on food as you travel.

Quite frequently, drugstores will have a small restaurant where you can also order coffee, tea, or other drinks, and light meals. Some drugstores even serve rather large meals. Open early in the morning and late at night, these eating places are convenient and inexpensive.

Tips are generally not required at these eating places such as cafeterias, where you serve yourself. At snack bars or drugstore restaurants, most people leave some small changes under their plates.

American Food Habits

Almost any bookstore has a variety of information about the restaurants and food specialties in the area. In addition, local newspapers and magazines include advertisements and articles about where to eat.

In general, American food is mild tasting; most Americans do not season their food to any great degree. Salads are very popular and are served all year, but especially in the summer. Waiters tend to assume that everyone drinks coffee, but simply tell them if you wish something else. If a waiter says "Now or later?" he means "Do you want coffee with your meal or after it?" Many, but certainly not all, Americans drink coffee or tea with their meals. Either way is perfectly acceptable. When dining out, you can ask for tea, milk, "coke," wine or beer if you prefer. Restaurants can only sell beer, wine, or other alcoholic drinks if they have a license, that is, permission from the local government to serve alcoholic drinks. Normally, when eating in a private home, it is consider better manners to take whatever is being served and not to ask for something different, unless the hostess gives you a choice.

The main course served in America meals is usually meat, fish, or poultry, but rarely is more than one of these served at the same meal. Seafood is sometimes served as a first course, however.

Most Americans eat breakfast and lunch quickly unless it is a social, business, or family occasion. The evening meal, however, is usually longer and a time for the family to gather together. Rushing through daytime meals is part of the fast pace in America. Another reason for rushing through daytime meals is that many people eat breakfast and lunch in restaurants crowded with people waiting for a place so that they, too, can be served and return to work at the proper time. So each one hurries to make room for the next person. As with busy people everywhere there is a real difference between a meal that is eaten in a hurry and one that can be enjoyed with friends during one's leisure.

Ordering Food

If you order meat in a restaurant, you will usually be asked by the waiter how you want it—rare, medium, or well done. "Rare" is not thoroughly cooked; the meat will be pink inside. "Well done" is usually very well cooked. If you prefer, you can indicate something in the middle by saying "medium," "medium-rare," or "medium well done." This applies chiefly to ordering beef.

When you order coffee, you may be asked "regular?" This means, "Do you want lots of cream in it?" If not, ask for "black"(no cream) or "dark" (a small amount of cream). Most often, however, the cream is brought separately and you may add as much as you like.

Coffee is the popular American drink at all hours of the day. You will probably need a few days to decide if you like it "black" or with cream and sugar. Other kinds of coffee, such as "expresso," are available in some of the large cities.

You will discover that American do not drink as much tea as other nationalities do. As a result, you may be disappointed in the quality of American tea. In public restaurants, tea is served by giving you a cup or pot of hot water with tea bag at the side. You can then make the tea as strong as you like it. In private homes, however, tea is frequently made with loose tea instead of tea bags.

Besides tea and coffee, other drinks popular in America are cola, milk and milk drinks called milkshakes, fruit juices, and other mild drinks. During warm weather iced tea is perhaps the most popular drink of all; others prefer ice coffee. You may notice that Americans drink a lot of water, sometimes with their meals. It is safe to drink the water anywhere in the country.

Bread and butter are usually served in restaurants whether you ask for them or not; there is no extra charge.

Eggs are a popular breakfast food in the United States. They can be boiled or fried, and served with or without a piece of meat such as bacon or ham. Fried eggs may be cooked "sunny-side up," which means they are fried in one side only, with the yellow, or yoke, of the egg showing. Fried eggs "over" means that they are fried lightly on both sides. Many Americans eat a large breakfast and consider two eggs and piece of meat a normal meal. In some parts of the country, potatoes are served with breakfast. They are called "home fries" or "hash browns."

With lunch or dinner, you may notice "French fries" on the menu. These are fried potatoes known as "chips" in other parts of the world. They are often served with the meal whether you order them or not. Another common vegetable salad served with lunch or dinner is "cole slaw," made from cabbage.

Two of the most popular American foods are hot dogs and hamburgers. You will find these available at almost all "fast food" restaurants. Hot dogs are also called "franks," short form for frankfurters. A hot dog is usually made either from beef or pork (meat from pigs), or a combination of the two, but a hamburger is beef. Both are served on a bread roll; hot dogs on a long roll and hamburger on a round roll. You have your choice of adding a number of sauces and vegetables at no extra charge. A favorite sauce of many Americans is a tomato sauce called ketchup or catsup.

When you are ordering your lunch at a "fast-food" place, do not be surprised if you do not understand the food orders—neither do Americans. For example, "draw one" means "pour a cup of coffee;" "BLT" means "bacon, lettuce and tomato sandwich." No one expects you to know this special vocabulary. Order your meal in the usual way. Eating places use their own special words to place an order quickly.

○ Words and Expressions

1. **wander** /ˈwɔndə/ v. to go around a lot of places or parts of a place with no particular purpose（无目的地）闲逛；游荡
2. **snack** /snæk/ n. a small meal or a piece of food between one's

meals 小吃；零食

3. **melting pot** *n*. 熔化锅(各种族融合之国)
4. **Never judge by appearance.**
   Never trust appearance. 千万不要以貌取人(物)。
5. **mislead** /ˌmɪsˈliːd/ *v.* to cause someone to form a mistaken idea or to act wrongly or mistakenly 误导；引错(路)
6. **outskirts** /ˈaʊtskɜːts/ *n.* outlying district of a city 郊区(常用复数)
7. **drive-in** /ˈdraɪvɪn/ *n.* restaurant, bank, movie or theater, etc. that offer service to people in automobiles 〔美〕服务到车上的餐馆和银行等
8. **surround** /səˈraʊnd/ *v.* encircle, enclose 包围；围住
9. **reservation** /ˌrezəˈveɪʃən/ *n.* an arrangement that a hotel room, restaurant table, train seat, etc. kept available for you 预定
10. **turn away** (*phrasal verb*) to refuse someone to admit 拒绝进入
11. **blend** /blend/ *v. & n.* to mix, mixture 混合；混合物
12. **grain** /ɡreɪn/ *n.* seed of cereal plant 谷物；谷类
13. **cafeteria** /ˌkæfɪˈtɪərɪə/ *n.* a restaurant or a dining room where people get their own food and take it to a table to eat 自助食堂；自助饭馆
14. **drugstore** /ˈdrʌɡstɔː/ *n.* store that sells medicines, soap, and many other stuffs (美)药店；杂货店
15. **cocktail lounge** a comfortable room in a hotel or bar where one can drink a mixed alcoholic drink 鸡尾酒屋
16. **specialty** /ˈspeʃəltɪ/ *n.* a kind of food that is always very good in a particular area, restaurant, etc. 特产；名产
17. **season** /ˈsiːzn/ *v.* to add salt, pepper, etc. to 加入作料
18. **a main course** a major part of a meal (usu. meat, fish, etc. with vegetables) 第一道菜；主菜
19. **poultry** /ˈpəʊltrɪ/ *n.* chickens and other birds kept on a farm to provide eggs and meat 家禽
20. **medium** /ˈmiːdjəm/ *adj.* of a size, amount, degree that is not small or large (大小，数量，程度等)适中的

Unit Four Food Customs and Eating

21. **apply... to** (*phrasal verb*) to be suitable or right in a particular situation or for a particular purpose 适用于；适合
22. **milkshake** /milk'ʃeik/ *n.* a drink of milk and usu. ice-cream shaken up together and given a taste of fruit or chocolate etc. 奶昔
23. **yoke** /jəuk/ *n.* the soft yellow middle part of an egg 蛋黄
24. **hash brown** a dish of chopped meat and potatoes 肉末土豆
25. **cole slaw** sliced raw cabbage 生圆白菜色拉
26. **frankfurter** /'fræŋkfəːtə/ *n.* cooked sausage 法兰克福香肠
27. **sauce** /sɔːs/ *n.* a thick, usu. cooked liquid put on or eaten with food 酱汁；调味料
28. **ketchup** /'ketʃəp/ *n.* a thick red sour liquid made from tomatoes 番茄酱

Content Questions

1. Why does the author suggest a visitor go out of the hotel and eat in the nearby streets?
2. What is America described as? And why?
3. What is the common way for most restaurants to draw customers into them?
4. What is the warning to a diner before he/she enters a restaurant in a city?
5. Why do restaurants on campuses and on the outskirts of towns attract students, drivers and motorists?
6. Why does a diner have to make a reservation for a meal in a restaurant?
7. How much does a meal cost a diner in a city restaurant?
8. What are served in American bars and cocktail lounges?
9. Where can a person get a quick and inexpensive meal?

10. What is American food like in general?
11. What does a main course include?
12. Why may a person feel disappointed when he or she drinks tea in America?
13. What are the other popular drinks apart from coffee and tea?
14. What are often served at breakfast table? How are they cooked?
15. What are the most popular fast food in the U.S.?

Questions for Thinking and Discussion:

1. How do Chinese food customs differ from the Americans?
2. Where do you usually go for a quick meal when you are out for business?
3. What is the big difference between Chinese and Americans in taking drinks?
4. What are the most popular fast food in China? Where can you get them?

2. Traditional English Food

English food, as we know it, owes a big debt to the Victorians. Like other northern European cuisines, it majors heavily on meats, dairy products, wheat and root vegetables and a diet conducive to manual labor and red-faced citizens. The nineteenth century idea of a varied diet was one with different sorts of meat in it. Milk and vegetables were regarded as not only uneatable raw, but highly dangerous until boiled thoroughly. To a certain extent this is understandable. In an era without refrigeration, when typhoid and cholera could strike even the wealthy, over-cooking everything was

Unit Four Food Customs and Eating

probably a sensible course to take.

The Victorian tendency to send splendidly choleric officials to war and rule over far-flung corners of the empire, and then later to retire them to the home counties, added a number of colorful foreign words to the vocabulary and foreign dishes to the table, which were gradually  adopted and anglicized. For instance, India provided the English language with curry, chutney and kedgeree while ketchup came from Indonesia. The aristocratic European tour also gave us the omelette, blancmange, marmalade, mayonnaise and macaroni to name.

In England we tend to underrate our own food, slighting our cookery because it is homely and familiar. We no longer recognize the traditional food we still eat as a cuisine or celebrate it and our food manufacturers make the great traditional dishes with microwave-ready imitations. Our enthusiastic adoption of foreign food, which has so enriched our cuisine, has almost made spaghetti the national dish. Yet a moment's thought can bring to mind traditional English dishes in everyday use which at their best can still impress foreigners, the sandwich, fish, pies like the cornish pasty, the Sunday roasts and their accompaniments mint sauce, apple sauce, cranberry sauce, horseradish, English mustard, Yorkshire pudding. Sometimes they have strange names Fool, Bubble & Squeak, Toad-in-the-Hole.

Out on the streets you will find everything but English food is available. You can find Chinese, Indian, Spanish, Italian, Greek, Japanese and other restaurants, but rarely see anything called an English restaurant. In fact, a visitor can try a traditional English meal with a family. This may consist of roast lamb, roast potatoes, peas, carrots and gravy, the puddings and cakes are the things that a foreigner will remember the most.

People in England have a special eating habit. Firstly, the main meal in England seems to be eaten in the evening. Secondly, a big English breakfast is not something that many English people seem to eat. Most of them have a light meal of cornflakes or toast and marmalade, orange juice and coffee rather than the eggs, sausages, bacon, bread, mushrooms and tomatoes.

◆ Words and Expressions

1. **owe a big debt to someone or something** (*a phrase*) to be grateful to; to have to pay（主要）应该……归功于；欠（债）
2. **the Victorians** people in the reign of Queen Victoria（1837—1901）维多利亚女王执政时期的人
3. **cuisine** /kwiˈziːn/ *n.* cookery 烹饪
4. **conducive** /kənˈdjuːsiv/ *adj.* likely to produce 有助于……的
5. **manual** /ˈmænjuəl/ *adj.* done by hands, hand powered 手工操作的；体力的
6. **typhoid** /ˈtaifɔid/ *n.* infectious disease marked by intestinal disorder 伤寒
7. **cholera** /ˈkɔlərə/ *n.* acute, often deadly disease 霍乱
8. **tendency** /ˈtendənsi/ *n.* a natural likelihood of developing, acting or moving 趋势；倾向
9. **splendidly** /ˈsplendidli/ *ad.* superbly, gorgeously 显著的；杰出的
10. **choleric** /ˈkɔlərik/ *adj.* easily made angry; bad-tempered 易怒的；性情暴躁的
11. **far-flung** *adj.* remote, far-distant 偏远的
12. **anglicize** /ˈæŋglisaiz/ *v.* to make or become English in form or character（在语言、风俗、文化方面）英国化
13. **chutney** /ˈtʃʌtni/ *n.* east Indian chopped pickles 一种酸辣味调味品（用水果、洋葱、辣椒等制成）
14. **kedgeree** /ˌkedʒəˈriː/ *n.* rice cooked with fish, eggs, etc. 什锦饭

15. **aristocratic** /ˌærɪstəˈkrætɪk/ *adj.* of nobility 贵族的
16. **omelette** /ˈɔmlɪt/ *n.* eggs beaten together and fried in a pan 煎蛋卷；炒蛋
17. **blancmange** /bləˈmɔnʒ/ *n.* jelly made in a mould with milk 牛奶冻
18. **marmalade** /ˈmɑːməleɪd/ *n.* fruit preserve, orange jam 果酱；橘子酱
19. **mayonnaise** /ˌmeɪəˈneɪz/ *n.* salad dressing made chiefly of eggs, yolks, oil, and vinegar 蛋黄酱（用蛋黄、橄榄油、柠檬汁等制成）
20. **macaroni** /ˌmækəˈrəʊni/ *n.* tube-shaped food made of wheat 空心粉；空心面
21. **underrate** /ˌʌndəˈreɪt/ *v.* to estimate too low 低估；对……评价过低
22. **slight** /slaɪt/ *v.* to treat someone or something as less important 轻视；怠慢
23. **manufacturer** /ˌmænjuˈfæktʃərə/ *n.* a person who makes things, especially in large quantity 制造商；制造人
24. **imitation** /ˌɪmɪˈteɪʃən/ *n.* things done exactly the same way as others, copy 仿效；模仿
25. **adoption** /əˈdɔpʃən/ *n.* taking or accepting something as one's own 采用；采纳
26. **enrich** /ɪnˈrɪtʃ/ *v.* to make something rich or better 使……丰富；增进
27. **spaghetti** /spəˈɡeti/ *n.* pasta in form of long strings, Italian flour-and-egg mixed noodles 意大利面
28. **cornish** /ˈkɔːnɪʃ/ *adj.* of corn or maize 玉米的
29. **pasty** /ˈpæsti/ *n.* (esp. in Britain) a folded piece of pastry baked with meat in it 馅饼；肉馅饼
30. **accompaniment** /əˈkʌmpənɪmənt/ *n.* something going together with something else 伴随物；附属物
31. **cranberry** /ˈkrænˌbəri/ *n.* red acid edible berry 酸果蔓的果实
32. **horseradish** /ˈhɔːsrædɪʃ/ *n.* cultivated plant with sharp-tasted root 辣根
33. **mustard** /ˈmʌstəd/ *n.* sharp-tasted yellow powder made from

seeds of mustard plant 芥末

34. **Bubble&Squeak** a dish consisting of usu. left-over potatoes, cabbages, and sometimes meat fried together 油煎土豆卷心菜；油煎菜肉

35. **Toad-in-the-Hole** (a British dish of) sausages baked in a mixture of eggs, milk, and flour 面拖烤肉

36. **gravy** /'greivi/ *n.* juices from cooking meat 肉汁；肉卤

Content Questions

1. What does English food usually major on?
2. Why were raw milk and vegetables considered uneatable in the 19th century?
3. What helped the English to add a number of colorful foreign words to the vocabulary and foreign dishes to the table in the Victorian time?
4. What did the aristocratic European tour bring to England?
5. Why do the English tend to underrate their own food and slight their cookery?
6. What restaurants do foreign visitors usually find on the streets of England?
7. What are the traditional English food that may impress foreigners?
8. What are the special eating habits of the English?

Questions for Thinking and Discussion:

1. Why are there so many loanwords in the English language?
2. Do you think it is necessary for a country to preserve its traditional food? Why?
3. What is a typical English breakfast and English high tea?
4. What are the similarities and differences in the English and the Chinese eating habits?

3. Dining with Americans

American restaurants are all the same. They prepare food in only three ways: boiled in water, grilled, and deep-fried; apart from these there is no other variety. Then, on the table a lot of "condiments" are served, so that customers can make things as sweet, salty, sour or spicy as they like. All over the whole country food stands on the street sell the same hot dogs, hamburgers, sandwiches, French fries, and so on. Wherever you go the taste is the same.

Especially for someone who has just arrived in America, the sight of a hot dog dripping with red tomato sauce and yellow mustard is enough to take your appetite away. But when you are hungry, there is nothing to do but close your eyes and swallow it. Hamburgers are even worse, semi-raw beef with a slice of raw onion and a slice of raw tomato, and then some hamburger sauce one dares not try it. Sandwiches sound good,  but are in fact tasteless. So eating is the most troubling aspect of living in America.

Being invited to dinner is a big treat for Americans, but I find it a painful assignment. First, I cannot get used to eating sweet and salty things together. Second, terrible-tasting food must be praised to the skies. Third, it is not filling, and you have to make yourself another meal after going home.

One time, a colleague said to my husband, "My father is a good cook and invites you two to have a taste of his culinary skill this weekend." It would have been embarrassing to refuse, so we had to accept. The meal turned out to be canned chicken with vegetables and rice, which tasted funny. Following this dish was a dessert of cored apples, stuffed with plum jam and coated in sugar. Eating it made me feel like vomiting, but I had to say, "Delicious! Delicious!" It was unspeakably painful.

Often when we were invited to dinner by Americans, I felt that they were not inviting us to eat but to look at the tableware. They do not use rice bowls. At the beginning of the meal the table is set with three plates, for each person, three glasses, a knife, a fork, a big spoon and a little spoon. The big spoon is seldom used, however, for they do not drink soup but lots of cold water, so the glasses see much service. The first course is usually raw salad or fruit salad, followed by bread and butter.

After that some strange-looking and odd-tasting little dishes are served while people eat and talk. Then comes the main course, usually a piece of chicken or steak or a slice of ham, with a few fried potatoes and some peas, or whatever, boiled to a pulp. When this is finished, dessert is served, fruit pie or ice cream, and cake, which is murder to eat, for it is tasteless. Moreover, it is not a lot food in the end, but a lot of dishes and silverware on the table. Last comes coffee or tea. American tea is a bag of tea-leaves in a cup of hot water, at which point, the dinner is considered over. Then you are invited into the living room to talk for two or three hours. The foreigners talk and laugh, and we Chinese do not understand what is being said. It is really unbearably painful. That is why I find eating American meals most troublesome.

Words and Expressions

1. **grilled** /grild/ *adj.* cooking on a barred utensil 铁篦子烤的；烤架上炙烤的
2. **deep-fried** *adj.* fried in deep cooking oil 油炸的

Unit Four Food Customs and Eating

3. **condiment** /'kɔndimənt/ *n.* flavoring, such as salt, spice, herb, etc. 调味品
4. **food stand** platform for selling food 食品摊;出售食品的流动货架
5. **drip** /drip/ *n.* falling of drops 滴;水滴
6. **take one's appetite away** (*a phrase*) to loose one's desire to eat 使人倒胃口;使人失去食欲
7. **semi-raw** /'semi-rɔː/ *adj.* half-cooked 半生不熟的
8. **a big treat** offering something special and enjoyable 款待;请客
9. **assignment** /ə'sainmənt/ *n.* work assigned to someone 分配的工作、任务、作业等
10. **praise something or someone to the skies** (*a phrase*) to express the strongest praise for something or someone 极力地吹捧;吹捧上了天
11. **filling** /'filiŋ/ *adj.* becoming full 填满的;充满的;饱了的
12. **culinary** /'kʌlinəri/ *adj.* of cooking 烹饪的;烹饪用的
13. **cored** /kɔːd/ *adj.* with the central part removed 去果核的;挖去果心的
14. **be stuffed with** (*a phrase*) to be filled, crammed, or packed with 塞满了,充满了
15. **tableware** /'teibəlwɛər/ *n.* dishes, bowls, etc. used on the table 餐具(总称)
16. **be boiled to pulp** (*a phrase*) (something) cooked to be soft, smooth, and wet 煮成糊状;煮成浆状
17. **silverware** /'silvəwɛə/ *n.* eating and serving utensils made of silver(knives, forks, spoons, etc.) 银制餐具
18. **unbearable** /ʌn'bɛərəbl/ *adj.* unendurable, causing a lot of pain and unhappiness 忍受不了的;无法容忍的
19. **troublesome** /'trʌblsəm/ *adj.* causing physical pain or problems that worry and upset someone 令人讨厌的;麻烦的

Content Questions

1. What are the three ways that the American people prepare their food?
2. What are the author's comments on the American fast food?
3. Why does the author dare not try the semi-raw beef?
4. Why does the author hate being invited to dinner by Americans?
5. What did the meal prepared by her colleague's father turn out to be?
6. How did the author feel while she was eating the dessert?
7. Why does the author think that being invited to dinner is not to eat but to look at the silverware?
8. What are usually served as the main course?
9. What are put on the dinner table as the last course?
10. What do American people usually do after dinner?

Questions for Thinking and Discussion:

1. *What is the major difference between the Americans and the Chinese in their ways of cooking?*

2. *How many courses do Chinese have at a formal (classy) dinner?*

Unit Five
HOLIDAYS AND THEIR HISTORIES

1. New Year's Day, January 1st

January 1st has been the first day of the year for Westerners for only about four hundred years, because in 1564, King Charles IV of France decided to start each year with January instead of with April, as it had been before that time. North America's January New Year's Day has its own customs, some brought from Europe with early settlers, and others "made in America."

The Pilgrim Fathers were the first Englishmen to settle in the American Northeast. They were Puritan Christians, who carefully followed the teachings of the Bible as well as some of their own even stricter teachings. They refused to celebrate New Year's Day as other Englishmen did. It was not a Christian holiday.

JANUARY—The month January was named for the old Roman religious god Janus. Janus was the Roman god of beginnings and endings. Janus had two faces looking in opposite directions, because he could see the past and the future. And January looks back on the past year and also ahead to whatever is coming in the New Year. The Puritans even refused to say "January," because of its connection with Janus. Instead, they called the first month of the year, "First Month," as do many Asian and other cultures.

Open House

  Other immigrants from Europe did bring their New Year's customs to North America. The Dutch first came to what is now New York, bringing their tradition of holding an "Open House" on New Year's Day, when the front door was left unlocked. Visitors could drop in without an invitation, talk a bit, and eat some Dutch cake, and help themselves from a large bowl of alcoholic fruit punch. Single men spent time at the houses of the unmarried girls on New Year's Day.

  It was in New York City that George Washington was officially sworn in as America's first President. While there, he found out about the Dutch Open House custom. And so he and his wife Martha held New Year's Day Open House in their official residence in Philadelphia, on January 1st, 1789. At later Presidential Open Houses in Washington, D.C., the President invited other government officials to stand in a line, shaking hands with each visitor. However in 1934, President Franklin Roosevelt discontinued these Open House customs because he could not stand up for such a long time.

  Many Americans now have a New Year's Day Open House, but in a much-less-formal way-inviting friends to drop by for a snack and drinks.

New Year's Day Parade

  Another immigrant group, the Swedes, brought two of their New Year's customs with them from Sweden. They dressed up in special costumes for a New Year's Day parade. They also ate baked ham on New Year's Day. Although some Swedes and others today may have ham on New Year's Day, there is really no special traditional American New Year's food. In fact, it's not a day for either a big dinner nor even for a family gathering.

  Like the Swedes, the English also dressed up in fancy costumes and went around their village at the end of the year, acting out the old stories of Father Christmas, of St. George fighting the Dragon,

Unit Five Holidays and Their Histories

and of others. But they only acted the stories. They made the motions, but said nothing. And so they were called "mummers," since to keep mum about something means to keep quiet or to keep a secret.

In early America on New Year's Eve, mummers dressed up and eventually formed clubs and marched together. In the 1800s, mummers in Philadelphia, Pennsylvania, used to end their New Year's Eve march at Independence Hall, where the new United States of America had begun. Big, noisy crowds met there, and as the clock on Independence Hall struck twelve midnight, empty guns were fired and everyone screamed and yelled "Happy New Year!"

Some years later, these Philadelphia mummers changed their parade from New Year's Eve to New Year's Day. And theirs is the most famous New Year's Day Mummers' Parade, with their own special music and marching style. Well, they don't really march. Instead, they do what is called a "cakewalk," with elbows pumping up and down, and bodies rocking back and forth, and strutting this way—a bit like some modern dance steps. So the Philadelphia Mummer's Parade grew out of an old European custom.

Rose Parade

But another custom, another even more famous New Year's Day parade is entirely American. Over a hundred years ago, in 1890 some people living in sunny and warm Pasadena, California (now part of the Los Angeles area) picked flowers from their gardens and put them on their horses and buggies, and on New Year's Day drove through their small town of Pasadena. Over the next years, this drive through town became a much bigger horse and buggy parade.

That was the beginning of the Tournament of Roses Parade, a New Year's Day competition to see which group, which business, which city, and even which foreign country can produce the most beautifully decorated floats-vehicles which are completely covered with plant materials and flowers. Each year the parade has a different theme which the designers of the floats follow. Some floats are built entirely by volunteers, maybe to tell about their city or school or organization. Professionals are paid to build other very elaborate floats which will advertise particular companies or places.

And now because of TV, this beautiful, warm, Southern California, flower-filled, two-or-three-hour parade has become part of New Year's Day, especially welcomed in the cold and snowy parts of North America.

In fact, most Americans begin their New Year's Day watching at least part of this Rose Parade. Besides the floats, there are many marching bands, people riding fancy horses, and other groups-all invited to take part because of their excellence.

Rose Bowl Game

Soon after the parade ends, there is the Rose Bowl Game, an American football game played by two university teams in a nearby stadium called the Pasadena Rose Bowl. The first game was held in 1902 between a California team from Stanford University and The University of Michigan. And the Rose Bowl is now a kind of national championship contest between two of the most successful university football teams. Every school hopes to have its team chosen to play in the Rose Bowl.

But besides watching parades and football on TV, or going to a friend's Open House, Americans do almost nothing else special or traditional on New Year's Day. They usually just rest. They need to rest, because most Americans have been up the night before celebrating New Year's Eve until long after midnight.

New Year's Eve

New Year's Eve is celebration-time for Americans, but not a family celebration. In fact, among the first English settlers in America, New Year's Eve was not a time of celebration. Instead, it was a time to think back over the past year, and especially of your sins and failures.

Resolution

In addition, everyone makes a New Year's resolution, a promise

Unit Five Holidays and Their Histories

to yourself to improve in some way. Nowadays, children resolve to obey their parents better. Adults resolve to stop drinking so much, or to control their temper, or somehow to be a better person. But sadly, most New Year's resolutions are broken by the second or third day of the New Year.

Church

Since most early Americans were Christians, they would go to church on New Year's Eve. In New York City many people would meet outside Trinity Church to wait for midnight. Many others would meet inside churches to hear someone preach about living a better life in the coming New Year, and then to pray to God, asking God to forgive past failures and to give them help in the New Year. This custom continues today primarily among Protestant Christians, who have a tradition of this kind of personal relationship with God. They frequently call their New Year's Eve meeting a "Watch Night Service," meaning that they will watch (stay awake) until the New Year begins.

Christian teenagers may go to a church recreation hall or to someone's home, perhaps to watch a Christian film, to listen to some Bible discussion, or maybe to pray, but mostly to have a party until midnight. Parents usually support such parties because they know that their children will be supervised by adults and will be learning something morally helpful.

A Date

But America now is far less Christian or religious than before, and so the majority of Americans, whether Christians or not, will have a New Year's Eve date. Couples will go out for the evening. They may be just beginning a friendship, or they may be engaged to be married, or they may have been married for many years.

And wherever they go, it is expensive. Most hotels and restaurants have interesting activities and special food.

In New York City

In New York City, couples may go to a stage play, then have

dinner afterwards in one of the many restaurants or hotels. From there they may go elsewhere to dance. And the man spends a lot of money at each place.

In the past, New Yorkers might end their evening in front of Trinity Church, but now they go to a special celebration not far away in Times Square. On December 31st, 1939, over one million two hundred fifty thousand people stood in Times Square to watch what still happens today. The large lighted ball at the top of a building slowly drops during the last few seconds of the year, reaching the bottom just at midnight, when the New Year begins. Immediately all over America people shout, "Happy New Year!", blow on special noisemakers, and then join others in singing the famous Scottish friendship song, "Auld Lang Syne". Outdoors, Cars blow their horns, church bells are rung, and, until recent years, firecrackers exploded. No one is expected to be trying to sleep at midnight on December 31st.

Words and Expressions

1. **Pilgrim** /ˈpilɡrim/ **Fathers** n. the first group of people from England who landed at Plymouth of America in 1620 一六二〇年移到美洲的英国清教徒

2. **Puritan** /ˈpjuəritən/ n. a person who is strict in morals and religion, who looks upon fun and pleasure as sinful 清教徒；极端拘谨的人；主张禁欲的人

3. **Janus** /ˈdʒeinəs/ n. ancient Italian god, guardian of gates and doors, beginnings and ends, with two faces, one on the front and the other on the back of his head 两面神

4. **Dutch** /ˈdʌtʃ/ n. the people of Netherlands (Holland) 荷兰人

5. **punch** /pʌntʃ/ n. a drink made from fruit juice, wine, water, etc. (果汁、酒、糖水等混合的)饮料

6. **swear** /swɛə/ v. (swore, sworn) to state or promise formally or oath 宣誓；发誓

Unit Five Holidays and Their Histories

7. **immigrant** /ˈimigrənt/ *n.* a person coming into a country from abroad to settle down there（外国来的）移民

8. **Swedes** /swiːdz/ *n.* the people of Sweden 瑞典人

9. **fancy costume** brightly colored, not ordinary clothes for special occasions 花哨的和别致的服装；假面舞会上的着装

10. **mummer** /ˈmʌmə/ *n.* a person in festival disguise 节日装扮的人

11. **yell** /jel/ *v.* to shout or cry loudly 大声叫嚷

12. **pump up (down)** (*phrasal verb*) to raise up (down) 抬上（抬下）

13. **strut** /strʌt/ *v.* to walk in a stiff, satisfying way 趾高气扬地走

14. **buggy** /ˈbʌgi/ *n.* a carriage 马车

15. **tournament** /ˈtuənəmənt/ *n.* a number of competitions between players who play the most skillful will win 锦标赛；联赛

16. **float** /fləut/ *n.* a large flat vehicle, on which there are special shows, or ornamental scenes, etc., is marching in procession 彩车；花车

17. **theme** /θiːm/ *n.* the subject of a talk or a piece of writing 主题；话题

18. **elaborate** /iˈlæbəreit/ *adj.* of detail; carefully worked out and with a large number of parts; complicated 精致的；详尽的；复杂的

19. **a rose bowl game** a postseason football game between specially invited teams 玫瑰碗球赛

20. **stadium** /ˈsteidjəm/ *n.* a large sports ground with rows of seats built around it 体育场；运动场

21. **Stanford University** a university located in Stanford of California 斯坦福大学

22. **championship** /ˈtʃæmpjənʃip/ *n.* a competition held to find the champion 冠军赛

23. **sin** /sin/ *n.* disobedience to God; the breaking of holy law 原罪；罪恶

24. **resolution** /ˌrezəˈluːʃən/ *n.* the quality of being resolute (being determined) 决心；决定

25. **resolve** /riˈzɔlv/ *v.* decide; determine 决心；决定

125

26. **trinity** /ˈtriniti/ *n.* a group of three;（in Christian teaching）union of three persons, Father, Son and holy Ghost 三人一组；[宗教]（圣父、圣子、圣灵）三位一体

27. **preach** /priːtʃ/ *v.* to give a religious talk during a church service 布道；讲道

28. **forgive** /fəˈgiv/ *v.* to stop being angry with someone or something and no longer want to punish them 宽恕；原谅

29. **Protestant** /ˈprɔtistənt/ *n.* (a member) of a part of the Christian Church that separated from the Roman Catholic Church in the 16th century 新教徒

30. **supervise** /ˈsjuːpəvaiz/ *v.* to keep watch over (work or worker) as a person in charge 监督

31. **morally** /ˈmɔrəli/ *ad.* in a moral manner 有道德地；正直地

32. **be engaged to someone** (*a phrasal verb*) having agreed to marry someone 订婚

33. **Times Square** (纽约)时报广场

34. **Auld Lang Syne** (苏格兰民歌)友谊地久天长

35. **horn** /hɔːn/ *n.* a musical instrument consisting of a long metal tube played by blowing 号角；喇叭

36. **firecracker** /ˈfaiəˌkrækə/ *n.* a small explosive charge used for making cracking noises on special occasions 鞭炮；爆竹
    firework /ˈfaiəwəːk/ *n.* device containing gunpowder and chemicals, used for making a display at night 礼花；焰火

37. **explode** /iksˈpləud/ *v.* to blow up or burst 使……爆炸；爆破

Content Questions

1. How did it come into being that New Year's Day falls on January 1st?
2. Who were Pilgrim Fathers?
3. Who was Janus? Did it have anything to do with January?

Unit Five Holidays and Their Histories

> 4. What do you know about the tradition of Open House on New Year's Day?
> 5. What New Year customs did the Swedish immigrants bring into America? 6. How did mummers in Philadelphia use to end their New Year's Eve march in the 1800s?
> 7. How did the custom of the Tournament of Roses Parade get started?
> 8. What do Americans often do on New Year's Day?
> 9. What do Protestant Christians and Christian teenagers often do on New Year's Eve?
> 10. What do the majority of Americans and New Yorkers do on New Year's Eve?

Questions for Thinking and Discussion

1. *How do Chinese people celebrate Chinese New Year Eve and New Year's Day—the Spring Festival?*

2. *What customs do you know are related to the Chinese New Year?*

2. April Fools' Day

The British and Scotch called April 1st "All Fools' Day," and brought their customs with them when they immigrated to the American colonies.

April Fools' Day is traditionally a day to play practical jokes on others, send people on fools' errands, and fool the unsuspecting. No one knows how this holiday began but it was thought to have originated in France.

The closest point in time that can be identified as the beginning of this tradition was in 1582, in France. New Year's Day was celebrated on March 25 and celebrations lasted until April 1st. In the mid 1560s it was changed from March 25 to January 1st by King Charles IV, but not everyone in France heard about the change, and even some who did know continued to celebrate the New Year in the spring on April 1st. They were all called "April fools."

Others, the more obstinate crowd, refused to accept the new calendar and continued to celebrate the New Year on April 1. These backward folks were labeled as "fools" by the general populace. They were subject to some ridicule, and were often sent on "fools' errands" or were made the butt of other practical jokes.

The tradition eventually spread to England and Scotland in the eighteenth century. It was later introduced to the American colonies of both the English and French. April Fools' Day thus developed into an international fun feast.

Each country celebrates April Fools' Day differently. In France, the April fool is called "April Fish" (Poisson d'Avril). The French fool their friends by taping a paper fish to their friends' backs and when

someone discovers this trick, they yell "Poisson d'Avril!" In England, tricks can be played only in the morning. If a trick is played on you, you are a "noodle." In Scotland, April Fools' Day is 48 hours long and you are called an "April Gowk," which is another name for a cuckoo bird. The second day is devoted to pranks involving the posterior region of the body. The origin of the "Kick me" sign can be traced to this observance. Mexico's counterpart of April Fools' Day is actually observed on December 28. Originally, the day was a sad remembrance of the slaughter of the innocent children by King Herod. It eventually evolved into a lighter commemoration involving pranks and trickery.

Pranks performed on April Fools' Day range from the simple,

Unit Five Holidays and Their Histories

(such as saying, "Your shoe's untied!"), to the elaborate. Setting a roommate's alarm clock back an hour is a common gag. Sometimes, elaborate practical jokes are played on friends or relatives that last the entire day. The news media even gets involved. For instance, a British short film once shown on April Fools' Day was a fairly detailed documentary about "spaghetti farmers" and how they harvest their crop from the spaghetti trees. Whatever the prank, the trickster usually ends it by yelling to his victim, "April Fool!"

Modern April Fools' Day Customs

Now April Fools' Day is mostly a day for children to play tricks on their friends. One is to secretly stick a sign on someone's back that says something like "Kick me" or "Hit me," but hopefully nothing derogatory or insulting (nothing bad).

For another joke some people get to their office early and set all the clocks ahead by one hour, and then tell everyone who come in the door that they are late for work. When they begin to apologize, they hear "April Fool!"

An April Fools' joke must always be done in kindness, and only to a friend. It should never be dangerous, never make the other person feel upset or angry, never physically hurt anyone, never damage anyone's clothing or property, never ridicule or make fun of what another person looks like or believes. It should be what is called "good clean fun."

On April 1st, teachers may give unexpected exam papers to their students. The questions on them make no sense, are impossible to understand. Eventually some students may find "April Fool!" written at the bottom of the paper, and begin to laugh, and then everyone realizes it is a joke.

Sometimes students have very cleverly found ways to play tricks on teachers. So, be careful. Some of these things might happen to you on this strange Western holiday. What are you going to do this next April Fools' Day, April 1st?

Words and Expressions

1. **errand** /ˈerənd/ *n.* a short journey made to buy something 差使；差事
2. **unsuspecting** /ˌʌnsəsˈpektiŋ/ *adj.* having no doubt about 不怀疑的
3. **obstinate** /ˈɔbstinit/ *adj.* stubborn; not willing to change one's opinion 顽固的；固执的
4. **backward** /ˈbækwəd/ *adj.* late in development 落后的；进展缓慢的
5. **originate** /əˈridʒineit/ *v.* to cause to begin 开始；源自
6. **label** /ˈleibl/ *v.* to fix or tie a piece of paper, cloth, etc. to something on which is written what it is, who owns it, etc. 贴标签；加标签
7. **populace** /ˈpɔpjuləs/ *n.* all the common people of a country 平民；大众；老百姓
8. **ridicule** /ˈridikjuːl/ *v.* to laugh unkindly at; to make unkind fun of 嘲笑；戏弄
9. **butt** /bʌt/ *n.* a person (or perhaps a thing) that people make fun of 笑柄；嘲笑的对象
10. **tape** /teip/ *v.* to fasten or tie something （用胶带）把……粘牢
11. **cuckoo bird** a gray European bird that has a call which sounds like its name 杜鹃鸟；布谷鸟
12. **prank** /præŋk/ *n.* playful but foolish trick, not intended to harm 开玩笑；胡闹；恶作剧
13. **posterior** /pɔˈstiəriə/ *n.* the part of the body a person sits on （幽默）臀部；屁股
14. **observance** /əbˈzəːvəns/ *n.* the keeping or observing of a law, custom, festival, etc. （正式）举行；遵守（法律、仪式、或习俗等）
15. **counterpart** /ˈkauntəpɑːt/ *n.* a person or thing that serves the same purpose or has the same position as another 相对应的人或物；对方仪式或习俗等
16. **slaughter** /ˈslɔːtə/ *n.* the killing of many people or animals 屠杀；

Unit Five Holidays and Their Histories

杀戮

17. **evolve** /ɪ'vɔlv/ *v.* (to cause) to develop gradually 使……发展；使……逐渐形成；进化
18. **commemoration** /kə,memə'reɪʃən/ *n.* the act of giving honor to the memory of 纪念；庆祝
19. **trickery** /'trɪkəri/ *n.* the use of tricks to deceive or cheat 欺骗；诡计
20. **gag** /gæg/ *n.* (*informal*) a joke or funny story （非正式）笑话；插科打诨
21. **documentary** /,dɔkju'mentəri/ *n.* a film, television or radiobroadcast that presents facts 纪录片；（电视或广播的）实况报道
22. **derogatory** /dɪ'rɔgətəri/ *adj.* showing or causing lack of respect 不敬的；毁损的

Content Questions

1. How did April Fools' Day develop into an international fun feast?
2. How do French people celebrate April Fools' Day?
3. How do people in Scotland celebrate April Fools' Day?
4. When and how do Mexicans celebrate their April Fools' Day?
5. What kind of pranks do people perform on April Fools' Day?
6. What rules should we obey when we play tricks on April Fools' Day?

Questions for Thinking and Discussion

1. *What influence do you think this Western holiday has on Chinese people?*
2. *Why is April Fools' Day so popular in the world?*

3. The Easter Symbols

Easter, chief festival of the Christian church year, celebrates the resurrection of Jesus Christ, and subsumes the Jewish Passover. Easter has been observed by the Western church since the Council of Nicaea, on the Sunday after the first full moon following the vernal equinox. It traditionally included a night vigil and the Baptism catechumens.

But Easter is now a festival less religious and most people in the western countries celebrate it just for fun and enjoyment.

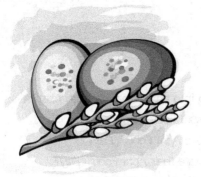

The Easter Bunny

The Easter Bunny is not a modern invention. The symbol originated with the pagan festival of Easter. The Anglo-Saxons worshiped the goddess, Easter, through her earthly symbol, the rabbit.

The Germans brought the symbol of the Easter rabbit to America. It was widely ignored by other Christians until shortly after the Civil War. In fact, Easter itself was not widely celebrated in America until after that time.

The Easter Egg

As with the Easter Bunny and the holiday itself, the Easter egg predates the Christian holiday of Easter. The exchange of eggs in the springtime is a custom that was centuries old when Christians first celebrated Easter.

From the earliest times, the egg was a symbol of rebirth in most cultures. Eggs were often wrapped in gold leaf or, if you were a peasant, colored brightly by boiling them with the leaves or petals of

Unit Five Holidays and Their Histories

certain flowers.

Two traditional Easter egg games are the Easter Egg Hunt and the Easter Egg Roll.

On Easter morning the children of the house join in a search to locate the eggs that the Easter Bunny had hidden while they were asleep. The searching might continue throughout the house with the older children helping the youngest. Sometimes prizes of candy are awaiting the child finding the most eggs.

Easter egg hunts are also part of a community's celebration of holiday. The eggs are hidden in public places and the children of the community are invited to find the eggs.

The rules of an Easter Egg Roll are to see who can roll an egg the greatest distance or can make the roll without breaking it, usually down a grassy hillside or slope. Maybe the most famous egg rolling takes place on the White House Lawn. Hundreds of children come with baskets filled with brightly decorated eggs and roll them down the famous lawn, hoping the President of the United States is watching the fun.

Easter Flowers and Easter Lily

Most cards have spring flowers. And these will be typical Easter flowers: those which grow from dead-looking brown bulbs: tulips, crocuses, and daffodils. The bulbs rest during the winter and then in the spring quickly shoot up their leaves and flowers, a symbol of Christ's resurrection from the grave.

However, the much brighter and larger white Easter lily is by far the most obvious symbol of Easter. And church will be decorated with these sweet-smelling flowers, called the "angel of flowers."

● Words and Expressions

1. **bunny** /ˈbʌni/ *n.* (a child's word for) rabbit 兔子
2. **Easter** /ˈiːstə/ *n.* the yearly feast day when Christians remember Christ's death and his return to life 复活节

3. **resurrection** /ˌrezə'rekʃən/ *n.* the rising of Christ from his grave, which is remembered with ceremonies on Easter Sunday, renewal (of life, hope, etc)［基督教］(耶稣)复活;复萌

4. **subsume** /səb'sjuːm/ *v.* to consider or include as part of something larger 把……归入;归纳

5. **Jewish Passover** (in the Jewish religion) a holiday in memory of the freeing of the Jews from Egypt 逾越节(纪念犹太人摆脱埃及获得自由的节日)

6. **the Council of Nicaea** The first ecumenical Council of the Church, called in 325 A.D. by Emperor Constantine to settle the doctrinal dispute between the Arians and the Orthodox, on the person of Christ. 公元325年,君士坦丁大帝在尼西亚亲自主持召开了基督教的"救世主教会议",确定正统教义,从而使基督教成为罗马帝国的统治工具。

7. **vernal** /'vəːnl/ *adj.* of spring 春天的

8. **equinox** /'iːkwinɔks/ *n.* time when night and day are of equal length 白天黑夜时间相等

9. **vigil** /'vidʒil/ *n.* (an act of) remaining watchful for some purpose(on guard, in prayer, or looking after the sick) 守夜;值夜

10. **baptism** /'bæptizəm/ *n.* a Christian religious ceremony in which a person is touched or covered with water to make him/her pure and show that he/she has been accepted as a member of the church (基督教)洗礼

11. **catechumen** /ˌkæti'kjuːmen/ *n.* a person receiving instruction in basic doctrines of Christianity before admitting to communicant membership in a church 新入教者;新信徒

12. **pagan** /'peigən/ *adj.* not believing in any of the chief religions of the world / 无宗教信仰的;异教徒的

13. **Anglo-Saxons** the people who lived in England in early times (from about 600A.D. to 1066A.D.) 盎格鲁撒克逊人

14. **worship** /'wəːʃip/ *v.* to show great respect, admiration, etc. to

Unit Five Holidays and Their Histories

God or a god (对上帝或神的)崇拜;敬仰
15. **predate** /ˈpriːˈdeit/ v. to write on (a letter, check, etc.) a date earlier than the date of writing 把(信件、支票等)日期填早
16. **wrap** /ræp/ v. to cover something in a material folded around (用东西)包;裹
17. **petal** /ˈpetl/ n. any of the (colored) leaf-like division of a flower 花瓣
18. **lily** /ˈlili/ n. a plant with large and clear white flowers 百合花
19. **bulb** /bʌlb/ n. a round root of certain plants (植物的)球茎
20. **tulip** /ˈtjuːlip/ n. a garden plant that grows from a bulb with large colorful cup-shaped flowers 郁金香花
21. **crocus** /ˈkrəukəs/ n. a small plant with purple, yellow, or white flowers, which open in early spring (英国的)报春花;番红花
22. **daffodil** /ˈdæfədil/ n. a yellow flower that opens in early spring 黄水仙花;旱水仙花

Content Questions

1. Why is there such a symbol as the Easter Bunny?
2. Why is the egg used as the Easter symbol?
3. How do children play the game of Easter Egg Hunt?
4. What are the rules for the game of Easter Egg Roll?
5. What is typical of Easter flowers?

Questions for Thinking and Discussion

1. Why do we like to have certain animals as symbols for some holidays?

2. What are the animals you know that symbolize something in Chinese culture?

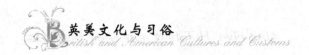

4. Traditional Halloween and Halloween Changes

The traditional Halloween you read about in most books is just a children's fun night. Halloween celebrations would start in October in every elementary school. Children would make Halloween decorations, all kinds of orange-paper jack-o-lanterns. And from black paper you'd cut "scary" designs—an evil witch with a pointed hat riding through the sky on a broomstick, maybe with black bats flying across the moon, and that meant bad luck. And of course black cats for more bad luck. Sometimes a black cat would ride away into the sky on the back of the witch's broom.

And on Halloween night big kids would dress up in Mom or Dad's old shoes and clothes, put on a mask, and be ready to go outside. The little kids had to go with their mothers, but older ones went together to neighbors' houses, ringing their doorbell and yelling, "Trick or treat!" meaning, "Give us a treat (something to eat) or we'll play a trick on you!" The people inside were supposed to come to the door and comment on their costumes.

Oh! Here's ghost. Oh, there's witch. Oh, here's an old lady.

Sometimes they would play along with the kids and pretend to be scared by some ghost or witch. But they would always have some candy and maybe an apple to put in the "trick or treat bags." But what if no one came to the door, or if someone chased the kids away? Then the kids would play a trick on them, usually taking a piece of soap and make marks on their windows. And afterwards they would go home and count who got the most candy.

One popular teenagers' Halloween trick was to unroll a roll of toilet paper and throw it high into a tree again and again until the tree was all wrapped in the white paper. The paper would often stay in the tree for weeks until a heavy snow or rain washed it off. No real harm done, but it made a big mess of both the tree and the yard under it. One kind of Halloween mischief. Well, that's some of what traditionally happened on Halloween.

Halloween Changes

But then Halloween began to change. For one thing, it got expensive. Younger children don't want to dress up like ghosts any more. They want to look like their TV heroes. So parents often spend lots of money to buy them Superman, Cinderella or dinosaur costumes.

Also, some older high school students have used Halloween night as an excuse for vandalism, spraying paint on windows, buildings, and cars, breaking tables in public parks, and so on. In some areas it's not safe to leave your car parked on the street on Halloween night. And then in the 1970s newspapers told of children coming home with dangerous things in their trick-or-treat bags, candy or apples with pins or broken glass inside.

And so, nowadays Halloween has become a time to be careful. Parents will arrange to go with their children to a friend's house for trick or treat. Or several families will hold a children's Halloween party together. No longer is it safe for children to go to a stranger's house for trick-or-treating. And elderly people are afraid when groups of teenage boys come by on Halloween night. Will they do some real damage? And for this reason, many cities have ordered all young people off the streets on Halloween night unless an adult is with them. So, much of the fun has now gone out of Halloween.

Adult Parties

But for adults, many hotels hold Halloween costume parties-with prizes for the best costumes. To look special, people may spend hundreds of dollars on an elaborate costume and mask. Other adults may wear a homemade costume to a Halloween party at a friend's home, where everyone then tries to guess who is who.

Cards

And adults do one more thing for Halloween. They buy Halloween cards to send to their friends. And the cards will have the traditional designs, ghosts and black cats and jack-o-lanterns. And, as for other holidays, all stores will have special holiday sales of anything to get people to spend money in their stores.

UNICEF Halloween

But something better has also happened to Halloween. Back in 1950 a Sunday school class in a church in Philadelphia decided that the Christian thing to do at Halloween was not to get something for yourself, but rather to share their "Trick-or-treats" with other children. Instead of the usual bags for getting candy, they used small boxes marked "Trick or Treat for UNICEF," the United Nations Children's Fund. As they politely went from house to house, they asked people not to give them candy but to put pennies (one-cent coins) in the box for UNICEF to send to needy children in other countries. They had a little rhyme, "Let's share, instead of scare."

That first Sunday school class got only seventeen dollars, but within fifteen years UNICEF had over three and a half million American children in over thirteen thousand cities and towns collecting donations—over two and a half million dollars. And the amount had been increasing year by year since then. Part of the popularity of the UNICEF Halloween Program was the early support from one of America's funniest comedians, Danny Kaye, who until his death in 1987 traveled at Halloween across America to promote the Trick or Treat for UNICEF.

Why did he do it? He said, "To help children acquire an interest and understanding of each other." And so, if some strangely dressed children come to your door some October evening and shout, "Trick or treat," you'll know what to do.

Unit Five Holidays and Their Histories

Words and Expressions

1. **Halloween** /ˈhæləuˈwiːn/ *n.* the night of October 31, when children play tricks and dress up in strange costumes 万圣节（10月31日之夜）

2. **lantern** /ˈlæntən/ *n.* a container, of paper, glass or metal that encloses the flame of a light 提灯；灯笼

3. **scary** /ˈskɛəri/ *adj.* causing fear（非正式）引起恐惧的；令人害怕的

4. **broomstick** /ˈbruːmstik/ *n.* the long thin handle of a broom 扫帚把

5. **witch** /witʃ/ *n.* a woman who has or is believed to have magic powers 女巫；巫婆

6. **ghost** /gəust/ *n.* (the spirit of) a dead person who appears again 鬼；鬼魂

7. **chase** /tʃeis/ *v.* to follow rapidly in order to catch 追赶；追踪

8. **mischief** /ˈmistʃif/ *n.* not serious bad behavior (of children's) probably causing troubles, or possible damages 恶作剧；调皮；捣蛋

9. **dinosaur** /ˈdainəsɔː/ *n.* a very large long-tailed creature that lived in prehistoric times and no longer exists on earth now 恐龙

10. **vandalism** /ˈvændəlizəm/ *n.* intentional, needless, and widespread damage and destruction, esp. of public property（对他人或公共财物的）有意破坏；野蛮行为

11. **spray** /sprei/ *v.* to scatter or be scattered in small drops of liquid blown under pressure 喷洒

12. **rhyme** /raim/ *n.* a short and not serious piece of writing, using words that end with the same sound 韵文；押韵

13. **donation** /dəuˈneiʃən/ *n.* the act of giving something (money or goods) for a good purpose 捐赠；捐献

14. **comedian** /kəˈmiːdjən/ *n.* an actor or actress whose job is telling

jokes and making people laugh 喜剧演员；滑稽人物
15. **acquire** /əˈkwaiə/ *v.* to gain, to possess with one' work, skill and action 获得；取得

Content Questions

1. What is the traditional Halloween you read about in most books like?
2. What were the people inside supposed to do when kids rang their doorbell and yelled "Trick or treat!"?
3. What changes do you know have taken place on Halloween night?
4. Why has much of the fun now gone out of Halloween?
5. What do adults often do for Halloween?
6. What does UNICEF stand for?
7. How did the UNICEF Halloween Program get started?
8. What should you do if some strangely dressed children ring your doorbell and shout "Trick or treat"?

A Question for Thinking and Discussion

Why have Halloween activities changed so much?

5. The Thanksgiving History and Modern Thanksgiving Day

Thanksgiving History

Many people think of Thanksgiving as a wonderful time of enjoying a long weekend, and eating a great dinner. Or, perhaps they view it as the start of the Christmas "Holiday" season. While these aspects may describe Thanksgiving, they are not the real meaning behind it. The American tradition of Thanksgiving can be

Unit Five Holidays and Their Histories

traced to the year 1623, the governor of the Plymouth Colony, William Bradford, proclaimed: "All the Pilgrims with your wives and little ones, do gather at the Meeting House, on the hill there to listen to the pastor, and render Thanksgiving to the Almighty God for all His blessings." The pilgrims were to demonstrate their gratitude to God for their survival.

They had undergone terrific hardships in their migration to their new homes. After sailing 9 weeks on the open seas, the 102 Puritans arrived in America on November 9, 1620. That first winter was very difficult and they were not really prepared for the hardships they were to endure. It was difficult for them to care for the sick because the sick outnumbered those who were healthy. By the end of the winter, many lives had been lost. It has been estimated that as many as one half of the Pilgrims may have died. The years that followed were filled with hard work and uncertainty. Still, they were comforted and encouraged by the Lord and were grateful for His blessing during those difficult years.

Over 150 years later, on November 1777, by order of Congress, the first National Thanksgiving was proclaimed and signed by the President of the Continental Congress. The third Thursday of December 1777 was designated "for solemn thanksgiving and praise." That with one heart and one voice the good people may express the grateful feelings of their hearts, and consecrate themselves to the service of their Divine Benefactor; and their humble and earnest supplication that it may please God, through the merits of Jesus Christ, mercifully to forgive and blot them (their manifold sins) out of remembrance. That it may please Him to take schools and seminaries of education, so necessary for cultivating the principles of true liberty, virtue and piety under His nurturing hand, and to prosper the means of religion for the promotion and enlargement of that kingdom which consisted of "righteousness, peace and joy in the Holy Ghost."

George Washington wrote a proclamation in which Thursday, the 19th day of February 1795 was set aside as a National Day of Thanksgiving. He stated that it is "our duty as a people, with devout reverence and affectionate gratitude, to acknowledge our many and great obligations to Almighty God, and to implore Him to continue and confirm the blessings we experienced."

On October 3, 1863, Abraham Lincoln and the U.S. Congress established the first annual National Day of Thanksgiving "on the last Thursday of November, as a day of Thanksgiving and praise to our beneficent Father who dwells in the heavens."

So it is that on Thanksgiving each year, Americans give thanks to God, acknowledging His blessings toward us throughout the year. Our gratitude is not directed toward our jobs, our successes, our material blessings or our health; but rather we give thanks to our God for the grace and mercy He has granted.

Modern Thanksgiving Day

Well, what happens on that day? In both Canada and the United States, the celebration is very similar.

Four F's

Food(Feast)—The food is similar. In fact the main items on a Thanksgiving Dinner menu written in 1863 in President Lincoln's time are the same ones eaten today in both countries—roast turkey with dressing, cranberry sauce, sweet potatoes, other vegetables, and pumpkin pie. Nowadays various salads and other kinds of pies,

Unit Five Holidays and Their Histories

especially apple and meatless mincemeat pies have been added.

But it is the bread dressings, the stuffing, that are packed into the turkey before it is cooked—that's what makes today's Thanksgiving Dinners different from place to place.

Food has always been the most important part of the Thanksgiving Day celebration. Thanksgiving Day is a time for feasting.

Family—The second important part has been family, going home to be with your parents or grandparents. And the third important part? Thanking God? No. No longer is Thanksgiving Day primarily a day to thank God, although most Americans will say they are thankful for their good life. If thanking God is not that important, then what is the third important part of Thanksgiving Day?

Football—These three all begin with the letter "F"—Food, Family, and Football, American football. All day long Thanksgiving Day, football games are played to be broadcast on television. The men in most families may watch football before the dinner, then watch another game after the dinner, and then watch one or two more games toward evening.

Friends—And there's another "F" in Thanksgiving. Almost anyone who is not able to go home for Thanksgiving and who has American friends will be invited to join some family for Thanksgiving Day dinner. Why? Just because Americans think it is terrible for any of their friends, the other "F" to have to be alone on Thanksgiving Day.

Thanking God—As always of course, believing Christians of all kinds will spend time that day praying to thank God. Those who usually attend church on Sundays may also go to a special Thanksgiving Day church service, perhaps on that Thursday morning or later that evening. For these people, Thanksgiving is still the kind that Presidents Washington and Lincoln expected it to be.

But for most Americans, Thanksgiving Day is very much like that very first one, a time for feasting, a time to be happy with family and friends, and a time for sports, with only a few thoughts about being thankful. Thanksgiving has become for most Americans a secular, family holiday.

But along with all of this, the beginnings of Thanksgiving are not completely forgotten. It is a time for remembering the Pilgrim Fathers in their tall hats and dark coats, with pilgrim women in their white caps and long dresses, with pictures of harvested fruit and vegetables, with vases of flowers, leaves, and clothes in the fall colors of yellow, brown and orange.

And it's a time to remember the native Indians like Chief Massasoit who helped the Pilgrims survive in the New World—with ears of colored Indian corn or stems of wheat for decorations, with Indian clothing and ornaments.

Words and Expressions

1. **governor** /ˈgʌvənə/ *n.* a person who controls any of certain types of organization or place; (in the U. S.) a person who leads administration of a state 总督;地方官;(美国)州长
2. **Plymouth Colony** a place where the first group of the Pilgrims settled down 普利茅斯殖民地
   Plymouth Rock The rock on which the Pilgrims are supposed to have landed in 1620 普利茅斯礁石
3. **proclaim** /prəˈkleim/ *v.* to make known publicly 宣布;公布
4. **pastor** /ˈpɑːstə/ *n.* a Christian religious leader in charge of a church and its members(esp. of a Protestant church) 基督教牧师(尤指新教)
5. **render** /ˈrendə/ *v.* to give (help) (正式)给予(尤指帮助)
6. **almighty** /ɔːlˈmaiti/ *adj.* having the power to do anything 全能的;万能的
7. **demonstrate** /ˈdemənstreit/ *v.* to show clearly 示范;说明
8. **survival** /səˈvaivəl/ *n.* the fact or likelihood of continuing to live 存活;幸存

Unit Five Holidays and Their Histories

9. **endure** /in'djuə/ *v.* to bear (pain, suffering, etc.) 忍耐；忍受

10. **undergo** /ˌʌndə'gəu/ *v.* to experience(suffering or difficulty) 经历；经受（尤指痛苦与苦难）

11. **outnumber** /aut'nʌmbə/ *v.* to be larger in numbers than 在数量上超过

12. **estimate** /ˌestimeit/ *v.* to calculate (an amount, cost, etc.); to form an opinion about 估算；评价

13. **continental** /ˌkɔnti'nentəl/ *adj.* related to or typical of a very mass of land 大陆的；大陆性的

14. **designate** /ˌdezigneit/ *v.* to point out or call by a special name 指明；指定

15. **solemn** /'sɔləm/ *adj.* serious; of the most formal kind 严肃的；肃穆的

16. **consecrate** /'kɔnsikreit/ *v.* to declare as holy in a special ceremony 献祭；奉献

17. **divine** /di'vain/ *adj.* holy, coming from God or a god 神的；上帝的；神授的

18. **benefactor** /'benifæktə/ *n.* a person who does good or gives money for good purpose 行善者；捐献者

19. **humble** /'hʌmbl/ *adj.* having low opinion of oneself and high opinion of others 谦卑的；恭顺的

20. **supplication** /ˌsʌpli'keiʃən/ *n.* the act of begging for help 恳请；恳求

21. **merit** /'merit/ *n.* deserving praise, reward; personal worth 优点；功绩

22. **blot** /blɔt/ *v.* to have spot or mark that spoils or makes dirty 玷污

23. **manifold** /'mænifəuld/ *adj.* many in number or kind 众多的；多方面的

24. **seminary** /'seminəri/ *n.* college for training clergy (religious leader) 神学院

25. **piety** /'paiəti/ *n.* deep respect for God and religion 虔诚

26. **nurture** /'nəːtʃə/ *v.* to give care and food to（书面语）养育；培育

27. **prosper** /ˈprɔspə/ v. to become successful or rich 繁荣；昌盛
28. **enlargement** /inˈlɑːdʒmənt/ n. causing to grow larger or wider 放大；扩大
29. **righteousness** /ˈraitʃəsnis/ n. doing what is lawful and good 正直；合法
30. **proclamation** /prɔkləˈmeiʃən/ n. an act of proclaiming 宣言
31. **devout** /diˈvaut/ adj. (of people) seriously concerned with religion （指人）虔诚的；诚恳的
32. **reverence** /ˈrevərəns/ n. having or showing a feeling of great respect or admiration 恭敬；崇敬
33. **affectionate** /əˈfekʃənit/ adj. showing gentle love or fondness of 深情的；挚切的
34. **acknowledge** /əkˈnɔlidʒ/ v. to accept or recognize 承认；以为
35. **implore** /imˈplɔː/ v. to ask in a begging manner (for something or doing something) 乞求；恳求；哀求
36. **confirm** /kənˈfəːm/ v. to support；to make certain；to give proof of 证实；确认
37. **beneficent** /biˈnefisənt/ adj. doing good，kind（正式）仁慈的；慈善的
38. **dwell** /dwel/ v. (formal) to live (in a place)（正式）居住；栖息
39. **mercy** /ˈməːsi/ n. willingness to forgive；not to punish 怜悯；宽恕
40. **grant** /grɑːnt/ v. (formal) to give what is wanted or requested （正式）准许；答应
41. **mincemeat** /ˈminsˌmiːt/ n. a sticky mixture of small pieces of dried fruit，dried orange skin，etc. (not meat) (葡萄干、干橘皮等)剁馅后做成的果酱(无肉)
42. **secular** /ˈsekjulə/ adj. not connected with church；not religious 非宗教性的；与教会无关的
43. **chief** /tʃiːf/ n. a head of a tribe 首长
44. **ornament** /ˈɔːnəmənt/ n. an object possessed because it is beautiful rather than useful 装饰品；装饰物
45. **paw** /pɔː/ n. an animal foot that has nails or claws （动物的）脚

Unit Five Holidays and Their Histories

爪；爪子

46. **handcraft** /'hændkrɑːft/ *n.* an object made with one's hand and needs skill 手工艺品

Content Questions

1. What does the Thanksgiving Day mean in the popular mind?
2. Why did William Bradford call upon the pilgrims to gather at the Meeting House?
3. What do you know about the first National Thanksgiving?
4. What did George Washington do with Thanksgiving?
5. How did the last Thursday of November become a day of Thanksgiving?
6. What are American people supposed to do on Thanks-giving Day?
7. What are the Four F's concerning the modern Thanks-giving Day?
8. How do devoted Christians celebrate Thanksgiving Day?
9. What do most Americans remember on Thanksgiving Day?

Questions for Thinking and Discussion

1. *Why do we say that Thanksgiving Day is a truly American holiday?*
2. *Do we have a day in China similar to Thanksgiving Day?*

6. Christmas, December 25th

Christmas celebrates the birth of the baby Jesus, the Christ Child. But who wrote down the date of his birth? Nobody. Who wrote down the year of his birth? Nobody. Then how did December

25th become Christmas Day? And more importantly, how did we get time divided into B.C. and A.D.? Well, let's start with the B.C.—A.D. question first.

B.C.—A.D.

As you already know, B.C. means "Before Christ" and A.D. means "after B.C."—something like that. Actually, A.D. comes from two Latin words that mean "in the year of our Lord." They are Anno, "year" and Domini, "belonging to the Lord," meaning "God." And so A.D. is the abbreviation for the time when Jesus Christ was living on earth.

Now one thing seems strange. There is a 1 B.C. year and a year 1 A.D.. But there is no year "0" because when the Christian calendar was first set up, historians thought that the year they called 1 A.D. was "the first year of our Lord," the year he was born.

Later in history, there were some changes in the Christian or Western calendar, and so historians today now think that the baby Jesus was born in the year 4 B.C. because that year fits best with the details of Roman history mentioned in the Bible's record of Jesus' birth.

Traditional Christmas

What we mean by an old-fashioned Christmas is a traditional New England Christmas. There will be snow. There will be a traditional white New England church with a Christmas wreath on the door or in the windows. There will be a bright blue sky in the daytime or a night sky full of stars. There will be people hurrying around buying gifts or taking them to friends. There'll be Christmas trees in each house by a window and candles in the other windows. It will be a white Christmas.

Decorations

Unit Five Holidays and Their Histories

Well, Christmas decorations are an equally big part. The windows of almost every shop or store in town, the inside of almost every office and department store, the city streets, the outside of public buildings and shopping centers—all will be decorated with Christmas lights and other decorations.

Christmas Lights

People like to decorate their houses or apartments with Christmas lights, strings of colored lights along the edges of the roof, or around the windows, or around the doors.

By the way, whenever most Americans see colored lights outside any building, they call them "Christmas lights" or "Christmas tree lights."

Christmas Cards

But in most homes there is one thing people have to do before Christmas—weeks before. They have to buy Christmas cards, address them, and mail them in time to be delivered before Christmas Day. And millions of Americans send fifty or a hundred or two hundred or more Christmas cards each year. About four billion cards are sent every year as Christmas and New Year's greetings.

Christmas Stocking

Children will choose one of their biggest stockings to hang up or maybe they'll use a special Christmas stocking—the bigger the better, since there's room for more gifts.

Christmas Music

The music of Christmas once was entirely Christian, with all the carols having to do with the birth of Jesus Christ. Starting hundreds of years ago, secular (nonreligious) songs were added which had nothing to do with the Christmas story. Most new Christmas songs now are about snow, Christmas lights and decorations, Santa Claus, and so on.

Christmas Symbols

For example, the holly tree has become a Christmas symbol since its leaves are bright green even in the winter and its berries are bright red like the blood when Jesus died. In fact, green and red have been the colors of Christmas decorations for hundreds of years.

But, even though these symbols of Christmas are still used, in most cases their religious meaning is either ignored or not even realized by most people. For most of the Western world, Santa Claus has replaced the baby Jesus Christ as the important person at Christmas.

Christmas Trees

One thing that most homes in America have at Christmas time is a Christmas tree.

In Hawaii people are using an artificial tree. And it can be used year after year, and it is cheaper than buying a live tree every year.

But most people really want a live one. However, as more and more people become environmentally conscious, they are buying a tree growing in a pot. Then after Christmas they plant it outside in their yard.

But to get a truly beautiful tree, you need to buy one that has been raised on a Christmas tree farm, where it has been grown and trimmed and watered for maybe seven or eight years or more.

But the favorite tree in America every year is a balsam fir, a tree with a special smell which most Americans now associate with Christmas.

Legends and Traditions

But why a tree at Christmas? Well, trees have always been given a special place in the myths, legends, traditions, and religious beliefs of people all around the world.

The Christmas tree really started in Germany. The Christmas tree was a kind of Christian hope for spring to come soon. Why? Well, first of all, Christmas Day comes right after the longest winter night, and people in the far north would soon expect the days to

Unit Five Holidays and Their Histories

become longer. And, of course, Christ's birth was associated with the bringing of new life. Second, an evergreen tree was eventually also connected by Christians with the idea of everlasting life.

In addition, Christians had for centuries honored Adam and Eve on December 24th by bringing into their house an evergreen tree they called the Paradise Tree. And they decorated their Paradise Tree with red apples.

Well, for some reason the tree was decorated and lighted, with other decorations added over the years. Little cakes, cookies, fruit, glass balls, toys, and eventually presents of all sorts were put on the tree.

And of course, Germans, when they came as immigrants to the United States, brought their traditions to America, including the Christmas tree.

Christmas Shopping and Gifts

Well, one important time comes before Christmas Day: The evening of December 24th, Christmas Eve. After work, you suddenly remember one more thing to buy for Christmas Day. People do last-minute Christmas Eve shopping before the stores close around seven or eight.

Then at home a husband might go to the bedroom where his children and his wife can't see him, and finish wrapping some of his last-minute gifts. While he is secretly wrapping the presents, his wife might be helping the children wrap gifts for him.

Once the children are finally in bed, the parents can bring out any presents which were too big to wrap up, like a new bicycle or an electric train set that needs to be put together before morning.

Christmas Day

Ah! Christmas morning! Children like to wake up early and sneak into the living room to check the presents, and then maybe they'll go back to bed and pretend they are still asleep when their parents come to wake them with a "Merry Christmas!"

Some Christian families have a tradition of reading the Bible story of Jesus' birth. Maybe it's to remind the children that

Christmas is Jesus' birthday. The children are more interested in what's under the tree.

Someone will begin to take the presents out from under the tree, see whose name is on the package, and then pass them around. Usually among the Christmas gifts will be some especially delicious candy or cake or cookies which everyone tastes.

Americans want to be home for Christmas. But most people will just watch TV. Well, most men will. The children may play outside or inside with their new toys, but the mother will be in the kitchen preparing Christmas Dinner.

Christmas Dinner is very much like an American Thanksgiving Dinner. For meat, turkey is the most popular. Then there'll be potatoes. Along with the turkey, there has to be the bread dressing made from small pieces of bread cooked inside the turkey. There will be cranberries cooked into a sauce, and its red color seems just right for Christmas. As at Thanksgiving, the dessert will be pie—pumpkin, apple, and others.

But only at Christmas will you have Christmas fruit cake, made with lots of little pieces of dried fruit and nuts. And if you are with British or Canadians, you may be served a Christmas pudding, much like a fruit cake, but with a different taste.

Christmas Dinner usually starts around one or two o'clock.

Friends almost never drop in to visit on Christmas Day, since it is a family holiday and no one really wants to be interrupted by someone coming to wish them a Merry Christmas. However, it is a long Christmas Dinner tradition for Americans to invite in someone who can't go home to be with their family for the holidays, usually a student or a single friend. In every university town in America, students from overseas will be invited to have Christmas Dinner with some American family, to share their joy at Christmas.

After-Christmas Sales

What about the day after Christmas? In America, most schools are on winter break, but everyone else goes to work as usual on

December 26th. Stores sell left-over Christmas items at half price and have special discounts on many other things.

Also, if you receive something for Christmas which for some reason you don't want, you can take it back to the store and exchange it for something else. All you have to do is show that it came from that store or company, even if you don't have the receipt.

Christmas Season Ends

When does the Christmas Season end? Most stores leave their decorations up until the end of the year, though some may take them down earlier in order to decorate for New Year's. For families the Christmas Season lasts just until they take down their Christmas tree, and different families put them up and take them down at different times.

Santa Claus Customs

Well, Santa Claus comes to homes on Christmas Eve all around the world. Nowadays you might find him in a home, quietly going about his job of filling the stockings that are hung here and there. How he got into the house, no one seems to know. But he certainly didn't come down the chimney and get his red clothes all sooty.

You might see him taking gifts out of his big bag and putting them where they'll be found Christmas morning by "good" boys and girls, along with gifts for everyone else in the house. At least this is how we expect a modern Santa Claus to deliver his Christmas gifts.

But you don't find Santa Claus just in homes and not just on Christmas Eve after the children are all in bed. Throughout most of the Western world, by the beginning of December you'll begin to see Santa Clauses here and there in the big department stores, at school Christmas parties for children, sometimes at office parties for adults.

In the United States every fall in some big cities there will be a Santa Claus College which trains men and some women so they can get jobs acting as a Christmas Santa. They have to learn how to put on their suit and whiskers, how to laugh like Santa, how to smile like a kind old man.

Well, why do people learn to be Santa Claus? They want some large store to hire them to be their Santa Claus during the Christmas holiday season.

Secular vs. Religious

But how did Christmas become the most important holiday in Western countries? Partly because the coming of Jesus was such an important event. Also, although the story comes from the Bible, many new and sometimes strange ideas and beliefs and customs have been added over the centuries in every country. And all of these are now part of Western culture. Many are secular, not religious. So Christmas is now a mixture of secular and religious symbols and ideas.

Commercialization

Every year some Americans will complain in the newspapers, on radio and TV, to their friends, to the stores, to the government that Christmas has lost its meaning. It has been changed from a quiet day to be with family to a whole month of Christmas advertising, Christmas sales, Christmas catalogs, Christmas letters, Christmas food, Christmas TV specials, Christmas parties, Christmas shopping.

Some Christians complain about these same things, not just because it makes the Christmas season so busy and commercialized, but mainly because the story of the first Christmas is lost. Most people in America have forgotten the Christ Child on his birthday.

The fact is that as most people in countries which observe Christmas have moved away from belief in Christianity and from belief in the original Christmas story, the commercial advertisers have found hundreds of ways to get those people to think about Christmas, but mostly as a gift-buying season.

Words and Expressions

1. **abbreviation** /əˌbriːviˈeiʃən/ n. a shortened form of a word,

Unit Five Holidays and Their Histories

often one used in writing (such as Dr.) 缩略；缩写词

2. **wreath** /ri:θ/ *n.* an arrangement of flowers or leaves, like a circle (one gives at a funeral) 花环；花圈（尤指葬礼上使用的）

3. **carol** /ˈkærəl/ *n.* a religious song of joy and praise sung at Christmas 圣诞颂歌

4. **holly** /ˈhɔli/ *n.* a small tree with dark green shiny prickly leaves and red berries 冬青属植物；冬青树

5. **artificial** /ˌɑːtiˈfiʃəl/ *adj.* made by man; not natural 人造的；假的

6. **conscious** /ˈkɔnʃəs/ *adj.* having one's mind and senses working; being able to think, feel, etc.; being aware of 有意识的；有知觉的；神志清醒的

7. **trim** /trim/ *v.* to make neat, even, or tidy by cutting 修剪；整理

8. **balsam fir** a tree with fragrant substance flowing out slowly 冷杉树

9. **myth** /miθ/ *n.* an ancient story, containing religious or magical ideas, which may explain natural and historical events 神话；神话故事

10. **legend** /ˈledʒənd/ *n.* an old story about ancient times which is probably not true 传奇；传说

11. **paradise** /ˈpærədaiz/ *n.* heaven 天堂

12. **sneak** /sni:k/ *v.* to go or talk quietly and secretly 偷偷地拿；悄悄地走

13. **package** /ˈpækidʒ/ *n.* a thing or things wrapped in paper and tied or fastened for easy carrying and mailing 包裹；包

14. **receipt** /riˈsi:t/ *n.* a written statement that confirms one has received money or goods

15. **sooty** /ˈsuti/ *adj.* having black powder in smoke 煤灰的；烟灰的

16. **commercialization** /kəˌmə:ʃəlaiˈzeiʃən/ *n.* something made to be a matter of profits 商业化；成为只为利润的事

17. **catalog** /ˈkætəlɔg/ *n.* a list of places, names, goods, etc. (often with information)（地名、人名、商品的）目录

Content Questions

1. What do B.C. and A.D. stand for?
2. What does it mean by a white Christmas?
3. What kind of lights are called Christmas lights?
4. What has happened to Christmas music over the years?
5. Why has the holly tree been taken as a Christmas symbol?
6. What kind of Christmas trees can be found in homes in America at Christmas time?
7. Why do American people have a tree at Christmas?
8. What does it mean by last-minute Christmas Eve shopping?
9. What do children like to do on Christmas Day?
10. Why do some families have a tradition of reading the Bible story of Jesus' birth to their children?
11. How do Americans usually spend the Christmas Day?
12. What is a Christmas Dinner like compared to a Thanksgiving Dinner?
13. Do Americans like to have guests at Christmas?
14. What can you do if for some reason you don't want a Christmas gift?
15. How do we expect a modern Santa Claus to deliver his Christmas gifts?
16. When and where do people begin to see Santa Clauses?
17. Why do people learn to be Santa Claus in the United States?
18. What do some Americans and Christians complain about at Christmas?

Questions for Thinking and Discussion

1. Why is Christmas becoming so popular all over the world?
2. What do Chinese people often do at Christmas?

Unit Six
SPORTS, RECREATION AND ENTERTAINMENT

1. Sports

Sports and recreation absorb a huge amount of Americans' emotion, as well as their time and, in some cases, money. "Sports" here refers to spectator sports, in which people watch others—mainly college and professional athletes—engage in competitive games. "Recreation" refers to leisure-time participation in athletics or other non-vocational activity.

Americans' interest in spectator sports seems excessive and even obsessive to many foreign visitors. Not all Americans are interested in sports, of course, but many are. And some seem interested in little else. Television networks spend millions of dollars arranging to telecast sports events, and are constantly searching for new ways (for example, using computer graphics and hiring glamorous announcers and commentators) to make their coverage more appealing. Publications about sports sell widely. In the United States, professional athletes can become national heroes. Some sports stars have become more widely recognized than any national leader other than the president. Some of them earn annual salaries in the millions of dollars.

What seems distinctive about American interest in sports is that it is not confined to particular social classes. People in all walks of life are represented among ardent sports fans. The collective audience for sports events is enormous.

Sports are associated with educational institutions in a way that is unique. Junior and senior high schools have coaches as faculty members, and school athletic teams compete with each other in an array of sports. Each team's entourage includes a marching band and a group of cheerleaders. In some smaller American communities, high school athletics are a focal point of the townspeople's activities and conversations.

Nowhere else in the world are sports associated with colleges and universities in the way they are in the States. College sports, especially football, are conducted in an atmosphere of intense excitement and pageantry. Games between teams classified as "major football powers" attract nationwide television audiences that number in the millions. There is a whole industry built on the manufacture and sale of badges, pennants, T-shirts, blankets, hats, and countless other items bearing the totem and colors of various university athletic teams. Football and basketball coaches at major universities are paid higher salaries than the presidents of their institutions.

In some social circles, associating with athletes is a way to achieve social recognition. A person who knows a local sports hero personally, or who attends events where famous athletes are present, is considered by some people to have accomplished something worthwhile.

Black Americans are heavily over represented in the major

Unit Six Sports, Recreation and Entertainment

sports of baseball, football, and basketball. While Blacks comprise about 12 per cent of the country's total population, they make up well over half of most college and professional football and basketball teams. It is not unusual to see a basketball game in which all the players on the floor are black.

The sport that is most popular in most parts of the world—soccer-is not well known in the United Stats. The most popular sports here are football and baseball games that are not played in large numbers of countries.

Meanwhile, one practical suggestion: Foreign visitors—especially males—who plan to be in the United States for an extended period of time will enhance their ability to interact constructively with Americans if they take the trouble to learn about the sports teams that have followings in the local area. Knowing something about the games and the players, and about their importance in the natives' minds, improves the foreign visitor's chance of getting to know "average" Americans.

The Sports Ethic

For hundreds of years, Americans were told "Do your best in sports, whether or not you win." Part of this sports ethic comes from the Bible's teaching that no matter what you do God expects you to do it "with all your might."

Another statement of this ethic is expressed in the Olympic Creed:

> The most important thing in the Olympic Games is not to win but to take part, just as the most important thing in life is not the triumph but the struggle.
>
> The essential thing is not to have conquered but to have fought well.

Sports Salaries

As various sports have become ways to make money, this earlier sports ethic is being replaced by the need to win, for winners make more money than losers. Professional players are now paid unbelievable salaries, more than the presidents of the biggest companies and much more than the President of the United States.

For example, in 1994, some huge American sports contracts were signed: In baseball, the San Francisco Giants baseball team agreed to pay Barry Bonds almost forty-four million dollars to play for six years, over seven million dollars a year for playing baseball! In basketball, Larry Johnson will be paid eighty-four million dollars by the Charlotte Hornets for playing twelve years, seven million dollars a year for playing professional basketball. The Cleveland Browns will pay Bernie Kosar twenty-seven million dollars for playing American football for seven years, almost four million dollars a year.

Children's Sports

A recent survey shows that most young American children enjoy sports, with boys more interested in team sports, while girls are more interested in individual sports. Of boys from eight to twelve years old, 22% like to play basketball best, 21% like baseball, 19% like American football, and 9% like soccer (international football). Of girls the same age (eight to twelve), 20% like swimming or diving, 13% like basketball, 12% like gymnastics, 12% like roller-skating, and fewer like ice-skating, softball, bicycling, baseball, soccer, or volleyball.

High School and College Sports

Both high school and college sports are called amateur sports because those who play are supposed to "play without pay," just for the enjoyment of playing, as the Olympic Creed encourages. Unfortunately, universities and colleges, have found ways to give illegal special benefits to their athletes.

The biggest problem so far has been with former graduates of

Unit Six Sports, Recreation and Entertainment

universities (now wealthy businessmen) who promise to help good high school athletes if they will attend their alma mater (their university), the one they graduated from. These alumni (these graduates) want their former school to have powerful sports teams, so some of them break rules and give money to important athletes. Schools which allow these things have been punished. They're not allowed to compete against other schools or to play in games that will be shown on TV.

Soccer (International Football)

In the past, few Americans were interested in soccer. In 1968 professional teams were organized, but they did not make enough money, and were disbanded in the 1980s. But in the 1990s many Americans became interested in soccer because of the 1994 World Cup competition in the United States. It's now the fastest growing sport in America, and is a school or after-school activity for both boys and girls, mostly in the fall of the year.

American Football

But all across North America, the most popular high school team sport in the fall continues to be American football. The team members are school heroes, and especially in the Midwest, the reputation of smaller cities and towns depends on the success of their high school football team. The teams have cheerleaders to lead the crowds in cheering their team to win, and the school marching band plays music to add to the school spirit. The same is true of college and university towns and cities.

Most American team sports are called spectator sports because people watch just a few athletes play.

Basketball

Even before football ends, basketball begins indoors, and is the main game played during the winter in America. In the Midwestern states, high school and college basketball is the topic of conversation in towns and smaller cities from November until spring. As with football, the prestige of the entire town may depend on the success of their high school team. And the same is true for college and university towns and cities throughout North America.

Also in winter there are indoor basketball games and other sports that are not just between high school and college teams. Many are just for fun as friends get together and play, maybe outdoors in the sunny southern states, like California.

Baseball

But the most important spring and summer sport is baseball, with professional baseball often called America's national sport. Baseball is sometimes called "hardball" because it uses a smaller and very hard ball. And this kind of baseball is primarily a spectator sport, with millions watching each game either in person or on TV.

Softball

But another kind of baseball is America's most popular participatory team sport, softball. It uses a larger, softer ball which cannot be hit so far. So there are softball diamonds in schools, towns and cities, where teams play in the late afternoon, evening, and at night under lights, as well as all day on weekends and holidays.

There are all kinds of softball teams. Most of the teams are formed in a town or community by people with some common interest, from the same company or the same neighborhood or the same club or same church.

More Americans of all ages play softball than any other organized sport, and primarily during June, July, and August. Thousands more who do not play come to watch their children and other relatives and friends compete.

Playing for Fun

In the "Special Olympics" and perhaps in community softball games more than any other team sport in America, the ideal of the Olympic Creed is most often followed. People play just for the fun of playing, and enjoy themselves whether or not their team wins.

The unfortunate exception, however, are some parents (usually the fathers) who forget that the sport should be fun for their sons or

Unit Six Sports, Recreation and Entertainment

daughters who are playing. They may criticize them for every mistake, or get angry at other players or officials when things do not go well for their own son or daughter.

Vocabulary Study

"To play"

By the way, in English the verb "to play" is used with only certain activities. You play football, play basketball, play baseball, play tennis, play volleyball, play golf-activities which have certain rules you must follow in order to win.

Some other activities use verbs, or are verbs themselves. You can box, jog, or run, roller-skate or roller-blade. You can swim, or sail, or hike, or hunt, or fish.

"To do" and "To go"

But you do gymnastics and body building, and you go rock climbing, mountain climbing, and bird watching. You also may go swimming, go boating, or sailing, or go hiking, hunting, or fishing. Most of these are only outdoor summer activities, except in Hawaii and the Southern States, where everyone is outdoors in their warm weather all year around.

Winter Participatory Sports

Popular participatory outdoor winter sports include the winter team sport of ice hockey, the individual or competitive sports of ice skating, and downhill skiing. Some people enjoy the individual or group fun of cross-country skiing, or the fast and exciting sport of speeding across the snow through the trees in a noisy snowmobile.

Sports Business

All summer and winter sports, whether spectator or participatory, are big business in America, not only because spectators buy tickets to watch such events, but because of the equipment and clothing the participants need in order to take part. They buy special clothes, shoes, and equipment for tennis, and entirely different ones for basketball, and still different ones for jogging, and very expensive ones for skiing, and so on. The companies which make the clothing, the shoes, and the equipment employ thousands of factory workers to make these things and thousands more people to sell them. Sports are truly big business!

Finally, to understand American culture, remember that Americans not only work hard, they play hard, and almost always just for enjoyment. And so, now you understand the importance of sports in America.

Words and Expressions

1. **spectator** /spek'teitə/ n. an observer of an event 观众（指比赛或表演）
2. **athletics** /æθ'letiks/ n. activities, such as sports, exercises, and games, that require physical skill and endurance 运动
3. **vocational** /vəu'keiʃənəl/ adj. relating to a trade or work 职业的
4. **excessive** /ik'sesiv/ adj. exceeding a normal, usual, reasonable, or proper limit 过多的；过分的
5. **obsessive** /əb'sesiv/ adj. of or like an obsession (a fixed idea from which one's mind cannot be freed) 念念不忘的；着迷的
6. **telecast** /'telikɑːst/ v. to broadcast a television program 电视广播
7. **graphics** /'græfiks/ n. the making of drawings in accordance with the rules of mathematics 图表计算
8. **glamorous** /'glæmərəs/ adj. attractive; exciting; and related to wealth and success 迷人的；富有魅力的
9. **commentator** /'kɔmenteitə/ n. a person who comments（实况报道的）解说员
10. **coverage** /'kʌvəridʒ/ n. reporting of events 新闻报道
11. **appealing** /ə'piːliŋ/ adj. attractive, charming 吸引人的；迷人的
12. **distinctive** /dis'tiŋktiv/ adj. having a special quality, character, or appearance that is different and easy to recognize 特别的；有特色的

Unit Six Sports, Recreation and Entertainment

13. **confine** /kən'fain/ *v.* to keep in a restricted space or within certain limits 限制在一定范围以内
14. **ardent** /'ɑːdənt/ *adj.* showing strong positive feelings about an activity 热情的；热心的
15. **an array of** (*a phrase*) a series of 一系列
16. **entourage** /ˌɒntu'rɑːʒ/ *n.* all those who accompany and attend an important person 随从；随行人员
17. **focal** /'fəukəl/ *adj.* of or at a focus 焦点的
18. **pageantry** /'pædʒəntri/ *n.* spectacular and impressive ceremonies or events, involving many people wearing special clothes 盛况
19. **classify** /'klæsifai/ *v.* to arrange systematically in classes or groups 分级；分类
20. **manufacture** /ˌmænju'fæktʃə/ *n.* the process of making goods or materials using machines, usually in large numbers or amounts 制造
21. **badge** /bædʒ/ *n.* a thing worn (usually designed on cloth or something made of metal) to show a person's occupation, rank, membership of a society, etc. 徽章
22. **pennant** /'penənt/ *n.* a long narrow pointed flag used on ships or by schools, sports teams etc. 长三角旗
23. **totem** /'təutəm/ *n.* image of a natural object, especially an animal considered to have special spiritual connection 图腾
24. **comprise** /kəm'praiz/ *v.* to be made up of; to contain 组成；包括
25. **extended** /iks'tendid/ *adj.* long or longer than expected or planned 长时间的；延长时间的
26. **enhance** /in'hɑːns/ *v.* to improve or to increase the good qualities of something 增强；提高
27. **constructively** /kən'strʌktivli/ *ad.* having a useful purpose; helpfully 建设性地；积极地
28. **ethic** /'eθik/ *n.* system of moral principles; rules of conduct 道德标准；行为准则
29. **creed** /kriːd/ *n.* system of beliefs or opinions 信条
30. **triumph** /'traiəmf/ *n.* (the joy caused by) great achievement or

success 胜利；成功（的喜悦）

31. **essential** /i'senʃəl/ *adj.* most important; necessary; indispensable 最重要的；必要的

32. **conquer** /'kɔŋkə/ *v.* to defeat (an enemy, a rival, etc.) 击败（敌手、对手等）

33. **San Francisco Giants** 旧金山巨人队

34. **Cleveland Browns** 克利夫兰布朗队

35. **gymnastics** /dʒim'næstiks/ *n.* a sport involving physical exercises and movements that need skill, strength, and control and that are often performed in competitions 体操

36. **roller-skate** /'rəulə-skeit/ *n.* a sport of skating with the type of shoes which have small wheels fitted to the bottom 旱冰运动

37. **softball** /sɔft,bɔːl/ *n.* a game similar to baseball played on a smaller field with a larger soft ball 垒球

38. **amateur** /'æmətə/ *n.* someone who does an activity just for pleasure, not as his job 业余爱好者

39. **alma mater** the school, college, etc. that someone used to attend 母校

40. **alumni** /ə'lʌmni/ *n.* (*plural form of alumnus*) the former students of a school, college, etc. 校友

41. **disband** /dis'bænd/ *v.* to stop existing as an organization （组织）解散

42. **the World Cup** 世界杯足球赛

43. **prestige** /pres'tiːʒ/ *n.* the respect and admiration that someone or something gets because of their success or important position in society 声望

44. **entire** /in'taiə/ *adj.* having no part excluded or left out; whole 完全的

45. **Special Olympics** 特奥会

46. **body building** 健美

47. **roller-blade** /'rəulə-bleid/ *v.* to skate on hard surfaces with a special boot with a single row of wheels fixed under it 滑滑板

48. **hike** /haik/ *v.* to take a long walk in the mountains or

Unit Six Sports, Recreation and Entertainment

countryside 远足
49. **ice hockey** a game played on ice by two teams of 11 players, with sticks and a ball 冰球
50. **cross-country skiing** the sport of skiing across open country rather than following tracks or roads 越野滑雪运动

Content Questions

1. What does it mean by spectator sports?
2. What do foreign visitors think of Americans' interest in spectator sports?
3. What do television networks often do to make their coverage of sports appealing?
4. Why are sports stars so popular in the United Stated?
5. In what way are sports associated with educational institutions?
6. What do we learn about high school athletics in some smaller American communities?
7. Why do we say that sports are associated with colleges and universities in a special way in the States?
8. What is one of the ways to achieve social recognition in some social circles in the United States?
9. Why do we say that black Americans are heavily over represented in the major sports of baseball, football and basketball?
10. What are the most popular sports in the United States?
11. What kind of athletic ethic is expressed in the Olympic Creed?
12. What is replacing the earlier sports ethic?
13. How do young American children like sports?
14. What problem do some former graduates cause to universities now?

15. What kind of punishment will a university receive if it gives illegal special benefits to its athletes?
16. What was and is the situation of soccer—the most popular sport in most parts of the world, in the United States?
17. What role do sports play in smaller cities and towns in the Midwest of America?
18. Where is the ideal of the Olympic Creed most often followed?
19. What sports belong to popular participatory outdoor winter sports?
20. Why do we say sports are big business in America?

Questions for Thinking and Discussion

1. What sports do you enjoy most? Why?
2. Do sports play such an important role in China as they do in the United States?
3. Do sports have anything to do with a country's economic, political and cultural situation?

2. Recreation

The word "recreation" brings to mind activities that are relaxing and enjoyable. Such activities as an evening walk around the neighborhood, a Sunday picnic with the family, and playing catch in the yard with the children seem relatively spontaneous and relaxing.

Much American recreational activity, however, seems to foreign visitors to be approached with a high degree of seriousness, planning, organization and expense. Spontaneity and fun are absent, as far as the visitor can tell. Many Americans jog every day, or play

Unit Six Sports, Recreation and Entertainment

tennis, handball, racquetball, or bridge two or three times a week, or bowl every Thursday night, or have some other regularly scheduled recreation. They go on vacations, ski trips, and hunting or fishing expeditions that require weeks of planning and organizing. In the Americans' view, all these activities are generally fun and relaxing, or are worth the discomfort they may cause because they contribute to health and physical fitness.

Much American recreation is highly organized. There are classes, clubs, leagues, newsletters, contests, exhibitions, and conventions centered on hundreds of different recreational activities. People interested in astronomy, bird watching, cooking, dancing, ecology, fencing, gardening, hiking—and on and on—can find a group of like-minded people with whom to meet, learn, and practice or perform.

In America recreation is big business. Many common recreational activities require supplies and equipment that can be quite costly. Recreational vehicles (used for traveling and usually including provisions for sleeping, cooking, and bathing) can cost as much as $35,000. Jogging shoes, hiking boots, fishing and camping supplies, cameras, telescopes, gourmet cookware, and bowling balls are not low-cost items. Beyond equipment, there is clothing. The fashion industry has successfully persuaded many Americans that they must be properly dressed for jogging, playing tennis, skiing, swimming, and so on. Fashionable outfits for these and other recreational activities can be surprisingly expensive.

A final point that astute foreign observers notice is the relationship between social class and certain recreational activities. In general, though, golf and yachting are associated with wealthier people, tennis with better-educated people, and outdoor sports (camping, fishing, hunting, boating) with middle-class people. Those who bowl or square dance regularly are likely to represent the lower-middle class.

Just as there are spectator sports and participatory sports, there are different kinds of recreation. Some are types of spectator recreation, such as watching TV or going to a musical concert. But these are usually just called "entertainment," because you let someone else entertain you while you watch or listen.

Many others are types of participatory recreation. A hobby is one kind of recreation that you participate in, and there are hundreds, maybe thousands of different kinds of hobbies and other kinds of personal recreation going on every day in America.

But now that video movies, TV, and computer games have become the "Great Entertainers" as Americans enter the 21st century, fewer people have the time to work on a hobby or to participate in the more traditional kinds of recreation.

Library and Reading

In early America, reading was the almost universal form of recreation, with a free public library even in small towns. Andrew Carnegie, an immigrant from Scotland who grew rich from making iron and steel, gave away 350 million dollars in the early 1900s for hospitals, colleges, and to build libraries.

But today, Americans do not read much, and so libraries are now more than just a place for books. You can borrow video and audio cassettes, use computers to find information, listen to lectures, see an art exhibit, or send your children to a "story corner" where someone will read a story to them, or maybe just part of it, so the children will then borrow the book to read and find out how the story ends.

Home Games

Also in America back before television, people played home board games, like chess, checkers, Monopoly, and more modern ones like Othello, and Triominoes, and others.

Unit Six Sports, Recreation and Entertainment

They also put puzzles together. Adults played cards, like poker and bridge, and children played simpler and faster card games like Uno. These are still fun, but now because of television and computer games, few families play board or card games together.

Arts and Crafts

Also before TV, Americans made things. Most boys made model airplanes or cars, and girls made clothes for their dolls. And as we grew older we learned arts and crafts, making things from common materials-toothpicks, and beans, or dry noodles, or seeds, or string, stones—almost anything. Now, adults make expensive things to use in their homes, to give as gifts, or to sell. And handmade Christmas decorations are the most important.

Some women and girls enjoy cooking and baking, and are so good that they enter their foods in competitions, like at county or state fairs, including fancy decorated cakes.

Gardening

Other Americans like raising house plants and outdoor gardening, and they produce attractive and beautiful landscaping around most homes in both poorer and wealthier neighborhoods. Even though these recreational gardens do produce fruit and vegetables for the family, it is almost always cheaper to buy the food in a market. But backyard gardeners insist that home-grown food tastes better, and provides relaxation and needed exercise.

Other Recreation

Some people take pictures, others play musical instruments, some raise pets, fish or birds or other animals. Some sew and do fancy needlework, and even display their work at fairs or exhibitions. Also for recreation, others like to eat outdoors at a backyard barbecue or drive somewhere for a picnic and some sightseeing. Others with more money, travel to places nearby or even around the world, some in order to learn something new, and others just to enjoy the sights.

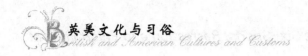

Shopping

But there's one kind of recreation which is very popular among American women. It's called "the mall crawl." They may spend a whole day in just one shopping mall, going from store to store, looking and perhaps buying. This is possible and comfortable because in or near all cities there are many huge shopping centers with large stores all under one roof, connected by walkways lined with maybe hundreds of open-fronted smaller shops.

These women just enjoy walking around and looking and shopping. Their slogan is "shop till you drop." Some of these just go window shopping, looking at what is for sale, but almost never buying anything.

Garage and Yard Sales

In the spring Americans often clean out their homes and garages, where they keep their cars and other things, and sell what they don't want. They may put them on tables in their front yard and have a yard sale. Or if it's too hot or rainy, they sell them from their garage and call it a "garage sale."

These sales are wonderful places to find used furniture, kitchen equipment, clothes, and who knows what? The slogan is "Our trash is your treasure." Newspapers have scores of advertisements for such sales every weekend during warm weather.

Collecting

But perhaps the most common American recreation is collecting, finding as many things of one kind as possible. And yard and garage sales are good places to find what you want. And for every collector there is a magazine or book about that hobby. Some people collect antiques—old furniture, old farm machinery, old cars, old bicycles, old books, old dishes, old, old, old anything, even old clocks. Some people's houses look like museums because they have collected so many old things. And some museums themselves have displays of collections that people began as just a hobby.

Others collect stamps or coins, bottles or bottle caps, stuffed

Unit Six Sports, Recreation and Entertainment

animals, postcards, matchboxes, photos of movies stars, buttons for clothing and interesting pins and buttons and badges. Some women collect certain kinds of dishes, like cups, or bowls, or all sorts of salt and pepper shakers.

  Knowing what a person collects is useful, since Americans like to give their friends something they like for Christmas or on their birthday. If a friend is a collector, you just look for something to add to his or her collection. Collecting can be a very expensive hobby, or it may cost almost nothing because friends keep giving something new.

Words and Expressions

1. **spontaneous** /spɔn'teinjəs/ *adj.* developing without apparent external influence, force, cause, or treatment 自发的
2. **approach** /ə'prəutʃ/ *v.* to begin to deal with something in a particular way or with a particular attitude 着手处理
3. **racquetball** /'rækitbɔːl/ *n.* a game played on a four-walled handball court by two or four players with short-handled rackets and a hollow rubber ball 短网拍墙球；手球式墙球
4. **bridge** /bridʒ/ *n.* a card game for four players who play in pairs 桥牌
5. **bowl** /bəul/ *v.* to roll a large heavy ball along a wooden track in order to knock down a group of pins 打保龄球
6. **expedition** /ˌekspi'diʃən/ *n.* a long and carefully organized journey, especially to a dangerous or unfamiliar place 远征；探险
7. **newsletter** /'njuːzˌletə/ *n.* a printed report giving news or information of interest to a special group 时事通讯
8. **astronomy** /əs'trɔnəmi/ *n.* the scientific study of matter in outer space 天文学
9. **ecology** /i'kɔlədʒi/ *n.* the science of the relationships between organisms and their environments 生态学

10. **like-minded** /laik-ˈmaindid/ *adj.* having similar interests and opinions 情趣或想法相同的
11. **gourmet** /ˈguəmei/ *adj.* producing or relating to very good food and drink 美食的
12. **outfit** /ˈautfit/ *n.* a set of clothes worn together, especially for a special occasion 成套服装
13. **astute** /əsˈtjuːt/ *adj.* able to understand situations or behavior very well and very quickly 精明的
14. **yacht** /jɔt/ *v.* to sail, travel or race in a yacht (a large boat with a sail used for pleasure or sport) 乘坐游艇
15. **entertain** /ˌentəˈtein/ *v.* to amuse or interest people in a way that gives them pleasure 娱乐
16. **universal** /ˌjuːniˈvəːsəl/ *adj.* involving everyone in the world or in a particular group 普遍的
17. **Andrew Carnegie** (人名) 安德鲁·卡内基
18. **give away** (*phrasal verb*) to give someone something without asking for any money 捐赠；赠送
19. **more than** (*a phrase*) not just 不仅仅
20. **video** /ˈvidiəu/ *adj.* of or relating to television, especially televised images 视频的；电视的
21. **audio** /ˈɔːdiəu/ *adj.* of or relating to humanly audible sound 声频的；音频的
22. **cassette** /kəˈset/ *n.* a small, flat case used in audio or video tape recorders or players 盒式磁带
23. **checker** /ˈtʃekə/ *n.* a game played on a checkerboard by two players, each using 12 pieces 西洋跳棋
24. **Monopoly** /məˈnɔpəli/ *n.* a card game 大富翁
25. **Othello** /əuˈθeləu/ *n.* a card game 奥赛罗黑白棋大战
26. **Triominoes** /ˌtriˈɔminəuz/ *n.* a card game
27. **poker** /ˈpəukə/ *n.* any of various card games played by two or more players 扑克牌
28. **Uno** /ˈjuːnəu/ *n.* a card game 优诺扑克
29. **craft** /krɑːft/ *n.* skill in doing or making something 手艺；工艺

Unit Six Sports, Recreation and Entertainment

30. **toothpick** /ˈtuːθˌpik/ *n.* a small piece of wood or other material for removing food particles from between the teeth 牙签
31. **fair** /fɛə/ *n.* a form of entertainment, at which there are games to play and goods to sell 展览会；集市
32. **fancy** /ˈfænsi/ *adj.* not ordinary; fine 别致的；花式的
33. **landscaping** /ˈlændˌskeipiŋ/ *n.* making the land around houses, buildings more beautiful by planting flowers, shrubs, or trees 环境美化
34. **barbecue** /ˈbɑːbikjuː/ *n.* a grill or outdoor fireplace for roasting meat 烤架；户外烤炉
35. **slogan** /ˈsləugən/ *n.* a phrase expressing the aims or nature of an organization, or a candidate 口号
36. **mall** /mɔːl/ *n.* a large, often enclosed shopping complex containing various stores, businesses, and restaurants 大型购物商场
37. **crawl** /krɔːl/ *n.* moving or advancing slowly 慢行
38. **trash** /træʃ/ *n.* worthless or discarded material or objects; rubbish 废物；垃圾
39. **scores of** (*a phrase*) a lot of 许多
40. **antique** /ænˈtiːk/ *n.* an object having special value because of its age 古董
41. **machinery** /məˈʃiːnəri/ *n.* machines or machine parts considered as a group 机器（的总称）
42. **pin** /pin/ *n.* a short, straight, stiff piece of wire with a blunt head and a sharp point, used especially for fastening 大头针
43. **shaker** /ˈʃeikə/ *n.* a container with holes in the lid, used to shake salt, pepper etc. onto food 摇动瓶；调味瓶

Content Questions

1. What comes to our mind when we see the word "recreation"?
2. What do foreign visitors think of American recreation?
3. What do Americans think of their recreational activities?
4. Why is recreation big business in America?
5. What is the relationship between social class and certain recreational activities?
6. What are the two types of recreation?
7. What is happening to recreation in the United States?
8. Who was Andrew Carnegie? And why did he give away so much money?
9. What games did American people use to play at home?
10. What crafts do women or girls enjoying today in America?
11. What do backyard gardeners think of home-grown food?
12. What is a shopping mall like?
13. What does it mean by "the mall crawl"?
14. What do Americans do with things they don't want in the spring?
15. Why is it useful to know what a person collects?

Questions for Thinking and Discussion

1. As college students, what do you often do for recreation?
2. What kinds of recreation do Chinese people often enjoy?

3. Entertainment

Americans who go out to eat or to a party on New Year's Eve,

Unit Six Sports, Recreation and Entertainment

most often go to restaurants and hotels that are advertised in newspapers and magazines, and on radio and television. Even though Americans probably watch more TV than most other people, they still read to find information they want. Most people even in this "Age of Electronic Information" still read newspapers and magazines for information and details.

Freedom to Publish

The Constitution of the new United States of America guaranteed everyone's freedom to publish anything, usually called the "freedom of the press," meaning the printing press. At first, many newspapers and magazines published wild, untrue stories just to get people to buy them. But soon new laws gave people the right to sue a writer or publisher in court for printing something untrue. A publisher  can even now print almost anything he wants to, but he may have to pay millions of dollars if he prints something which he should know is not true and which hurts another person. So today, the American press has become more reliable.

Reading is one kind of entertainment. Newspapers and magazines are often called the "print media," meaning that they are one medium to carry information. But the print media do not operate just to entertain people with interesting news and beautiful pictures. They exist to make money.

Newspapers

Big, thick newspapers and magazines are sold in America very cheaply because most publishers make their money from selling advertising space to businesses. And on Sundays most newspapers include their own kind of brightly colored magazine, with lots of expensive advertising. They must sell advertising space to survive.

By the way, the United States Government is one of the largest publishers in the United States, but it is not allowed to produce any newspaper or news magazine to be sold or given to the general American public. However, various government departments provide free materials to help in completing tax forms, advice on how to buy a used car, reports of scientific research done by government scientists, and so on. Each state prints many things to promote their state as a good place to visit, to live, and to do business.

Of course, the owners of each newspaper and magazine can influence what will be printed. So when we read a newspaper or magazine, we try to remember whether it is a conservative or liberal, Democratic or Republican, pro-union or pro-management one and so on.

Government cannot control what a newspaper chooses to print unless the Congress has passed a law making something illegal. In fact, the late President Richard Nixon resigned primarily because reporters for the *Washington Post* newspaper showed that the President had lied when he was asked about the Watergate burglary.

Although the *Washington Post* is one of America's most respected newspapers, few people outside of Washington, D. C. , read it. Each big city has its own newspapers, but only the *New York Times* is widely read outside its "home area." Only specialized papers are read nationwide, such as the *Wall Street Journal*, which has mostly financial information, and now an Asian edition. Actually, until the 1980s America had no truly national newspaper.

Local newspapers are usually delivered to each subscriber's home or office by a delivery person. Many Americans get their first jobs delivering papers to homes. They get up early every morning, go and get some newspapers from the dealer, and then carry them to the houses on their paper route.

Newspapers are found on many street corners in vending machines, each kind in its own separate box. To buy a paper you just put a coin in the coin slot to unlock the door.

Unit Six Sports, Recreation and Entertainment

Magazines

Magazines are almost never sold in vending machines, but rather at magazine stands or in supermarkets and other stores—hundreds of monthly magazines on all subjects. And although they are colorful and very expensive to produce, the advertising keeps the price low, from under one dollar to maybe as much as five dollars. The monthly magazines with the greatest sales are almost all for women because nearly half of American women are home all day each day with time to read. Men buy lots of sports magazines, and teenagers buy movie and music magazines.

Weekly news magazines are read by better-educated Americans, and give more news than most newspapers or TV do. TV Guide is a popular weekly magazine with just a few stories but lots of information about the programs that will be shown that week on TV. But still, the monthly magazine which for many years has had the most readers in America can be enjoyed by anyone who has finished high school—the *Reader's Digest*, with international and other language editions around the world.

The print media has always been important in America. In 1787, Thomas Jefferson, America's third President, wrote about the importance of newspapers for American freedom:

> The basis of our government being the opinion of the people, the very first object should be to keep that right; and were it left to me to decide whether we should have a government without newspapers, or newspapers without a government, I should not hesitate a moment to prefer the latter.

Jefferson would rather have newspapers without government than government without newspapers. Americans expect the press to be like a watchdog, warning them of problems.

So America's print media are not only for entertainment, but they are a necessary source of information.

The Broadcasting Media

America has not only the print media but the broadcast media of radio and television (TV), and also the film industry. When these were first invented, they had the same freedom as newspapers. They could say or show whatever they wanted to.

But although the government cannot regulate program content, it can say when certain things can be broadcast. Programs with swearing and so-called dirty language, or with much violence or sex can be broadcast, but usually only late at night so children will not watch.

But the broadcast media wants freedom to show what modern American society is like, and what Americans want to see or hear. They say that the homes, the churches, and the schools, and not the media, should be responsible to improve society. Some Americans support the broadcasters' right of free speech. But other Americans strongly disagree and want restrictions on TV violence and sex. And Americans struggle to find a balance between the right to discuss and show everything, and the need for moral standards in society.

Some groups blame the media for causing social problems because people imitate what they see and hear. Media people say that they are only reporting what is already happening.

Most people, of course, are more curious about the bad in society than about the good, and so the media can make more money if they present the bad.

Entertainment, especially in America, is big business because each type of entertainment is expensive to produce. In some English-speaking countries the government has its own radio and TV stations. However, in the United States, no part of the government is allowed to produce newspapers or magazines or films, or to operate a radio or TV station to reach the American people. Americans fear that the government might use this to influence voters in future elections. The Voice of America does broadcast to overseas listeners but not to people in the United States.

Unit Six Sports, Recreation and Entertainment

Radio

The Radio Corporation of America (RCA) was formed in 1919 to send telegrams by radio across the Atlantic Ocean. Its commercial manager David Sarnoff worked to start a national radio broadcasting network. And in 1926 RCA established the National Broadcasting Corporation (NBC), with its headquarters in New York City.

NBC was America's first commercial radio network, connecting to broadcasting stations across the country by special lines. The next year in 1927, the Columbia Broadcasting System (CBS) began as the second network.

Originally radio stations broadcast only live music. And in 1933, NBC formed its own NBC Symphony Orchestra. NBC had earlier started to switch from all-music to entertainment, first with comedy shows and tried to give Americans something to laugh about during the difficult years of the Great Depression.

In 1935 Sarnoff announced that RCA would introduce a system for not only hearing but seeing a performance broadcast through the air-television. In 1939 President Roosevelt spoke on experimental television at the New York City World's Fair, the first President to be on TV.

In 1941, NBC sold one of its two networks, and it became the third major commercial broadcasting network in the United States, the American Broadcasting Company (ABC).

Then as television became popular, it became the source of information and entertainment for most American homes. And so radio stations broke away from the three networks and focused on their local area, changing to maybe just one kind of music, or to call-in talk shows, where the listeners telephone the station and talk with the host. Some stations now broadcast only in Spanish or other languages. Some have only news 24 hours a day, and others provide just religious programs.

And now America has no national commercial radio networks. Instead, there are about ten thousand individual radio stations across the country.

But there are two new non-commercial public radio networks—National Public Radio (NPR) providing news and information, and American Public Radio (APR) with music and cultural programs. Their programs go to hundreds of non-profit, publicly supported stations broadcasting from universities, colleges, and independent locations.

Television

The three commercial radio stations (networks), ABC, CBS, and NBC, soon started television networks. And with the coming of television not only did radio lose many listeners, fewer Americans went to the movies, to see films in theaters.

By the way, in America, radio and television are broadcast free to the user, with no tax on radios or TV's, as in some countries. To earn money then, each broadcaster charges for its commercial advertising time. And the cost of advertising depends on how many people tune to a particular program—how many people will receive the advertiser's message.

At first the motion picture studios refused to allow television networks to broadcast any films. But after the ABC network merged with United Paramount Theatres, ABC-Television began programs especially for children and young people, like "The Mickey Mouse Club." They were produced by Paramount. And today production of TV programs is the biggest business in Hollywood, not films to show in theaters.

The years 1954 to 1959 were the "Golden Years of Television," as networks produced high quality entertainment—dramas, comedies, the arts, and in-depth news reports. But then serious television gave way to what the public wanted to see—game shows, where people won huge amounts of money primarily for answering questions. However, in 1959 it was discovered that some of the game shows had been "fixed" (the winners had been given secret help to win), and these shows lost their popularity.

The late 1950s were also the years of the popular situation comedies

Unit Six Sports, Recreation and Entertainment

("sit-coms"), which each week showed the same people in new situations which were funny. "I Love Lucy" was successful on CBS, and because it was on film, it could be rerun every few years. But everything was still in black and white. Then RCA and NBC brought color to television in 1964. And within ten years, television was reflecting what was happening in American society—in color. Sit-coms with a social message brought CBS to the top of the "ratings," the number of households watching their programs. And it remained the most popular TV network until 1985, when NBC won out with "The Cosby Show", about a successful middle-class Black family.

A new TV company became important in the mid 1990s, Fox Broadcasting. In 1994 Fox-TV controlled 188 stations, while ABC-TV had 225, CBS-TV had 215, and NBC-TV had 214—all together about 850 different stations across the United States controlled by just these four networks. And Fox hopes to soon be the fourth major American TV broadcasting network, especially since it bought the rights to broadcast the National Football League games for four years-and paid $1.6 billion dollars.

An alternative to broadcast TV is cable television, which reaches over 55 million American homes twenty-four hours a day. Each subscriber pays each month for this service and can choose from maybe 24 different channels showing old or new movies, the Disney programs, Cable News Network (CNN), and others.

Movies

The other huge entertainment industry in America is, of course, film making. From the early days of the black-and-white silent films, the American film makers in Hollywood, California, have been world leaders, or at least the leaders in making money from films. In the early days, many Americans went to the movies once a week. Southern California not only has highly skilled technicians, but its year-round sunny weather and its nearby mountains, deserts, ocean, farms, and city neighborhoods are ideal for making motion pictures. And Hollywood makes more than just entertainment films.

In the early days of film making, the studios agreed together about what things they would not show. However after World War II, changes came more rapidly in the film industry, partly because society itself was changing so fast. The types of films which people would go to see were no longer primarily the "happy ending" films. Instead, the films that became popular showed more fighting, more lawbreaking, and more immorality. The studios made many of these films because they made more money for the theaters. But when many people complained, some communities passed laws that stopped their theaters from showing certain films.

Ratings of Movies

To guide people in choosing which films to see, the film industry set up film ratings, based on how much violence, how much sex, and how much bad language was shown. A "G" film was for a "general" audience, including young children. Some were not recommended for young children. For some others, parents were warned to decide first whether the films were suitable for their children. For others, no one under 18 years of age was allowed to watch. These were just guidelines, and over the years even some so-called "G" films became too violent or too frightening for very young children.

But by the late 1990s Americans no longer regularly went to see films in the theater, partly because of the high cost of tickets, partly because TV was popular, partly because video movies could be rented cheaply, but mostly because people just did not like most of the films being made.

Problems

Instead of movies, television has become the "Great Entertainer" of modern America, with children watching so much TV that they neglect school homework, sports, hobbies, and especially reading. Teachers and many parents feel that TV is bad for the children of America, regardless of how good or bad the programs themselves might be. During the early evening, broadcasters are supposed to show only programs which are suitable

Unit Six Sports, Recreation and Entertainment

for children. But TV programs become more and more violent and immoral, even during the early evening family time.

And in the early 1990s people formed groups to get TV violence reduced. One sometimes effective way is to write to a company and complain about violence on the programs they help to support with their advertising.

Then because of more public pressure, broadcasters themselves agreed in 1994 to reduce TV and movie violence because the United States Congress was considering laws to control what is shown on TV. However, unless many more Americans decide not to watch violence, any further changes will probably come only very slowly.

Benefits

But TV has done some good things in the United States. Because of television, modern American children are far more aware of nature, the environment, space travel, world affairs, and politics than their parents were at the same age. But some critics argue that much of this is only awareness, not thoughtful understanding, not true knowledge.

One basic disagreement still exists. Concerned parents and leaders in education, churches, and government feel that the entertainment industries are causing a decline in American social morality and therefore should be controlled. The industry leaders disagree, saying that their films and programs only show what is already happening in American society.

But regardless of the outcome—radio, television, and films will continue to be the basic forms of entertainment in America.

● Words and Expressions

1. **constitution** /ˌkɔnstiˈtjuːʃən/ *n.* the basic principles and laws of a nation or a state that determine the powers and duties of the government and guarantee certain rights to the people in it 宪法
2. **guarantee** /ˌɡærənˈtiː/ *v.* to promise to do something or promise

that something will happen 保证

3. **promote** /prə'məut/ *v.* to help actively in forming, arranging, or encouraging 积极筹划或促进

4. **conservative** /kən'sə:vətiv/ *adj.* favoring traditional views and values 保守的

5. **liberal** /'libərəl/ *adj.* open to new ideas for progress 自由主义的;开明的

6. **democratic** /ˌdemə'krætik/ *adj.* of or characterized by democracy, or advocating democracy 民主的

7. **republican** /ri'pʌblikən/ *adj.* of, relating to, or characteristic of a republic 共和主义的

8. **pro-union** /prəu-'ju:njən/ *adj.* in favor of a labor union 亲劳方的

9. **pro-management** /prəu-'mænidʒmənt/ *adj.* in favor of persons who control or direct a business 亲资方的

10. **late** /leit/ *adj.* dead 已故的

11. **Richard Nixon** 理查德·尼克松(美国总统1968—1974)

12. **resign** /ri'zain/ *v.* to give up (a position), especially formally 辞职

13. ***Washington Post*** 华盛顿邮报

14. **Washington, D. C.** 华盛顿特区

15. ***New York Times*** 纽约时报

16. **subscriber** /sʌbs'kraibə/ *n.* someone who pays money, usually once a year, to receive copies of a newspaper or magazine, or to receive service 订户

17. **dealer** /'di:lə/ *n.* someone who is engaged in buying and selling 经销商

18. **vend** /vend/ *v.* to sell by means of a vending machine or by peddling 用售货机出售;叫卖

19. **slot** /slɔt/ *n.* a narrow opening 狭窄的开口

20. **stand** /stænd/ *n.* a booth, stall, or counter for the display of goods for sale 售货亭;摊位;柜台

21. ***Reader's Digest*** 读者文摘(杂志)

Unit Six Sports, Recreation and Entertainment

22. **edition** /iˈdiʃən/ *n.* the form that a book, newspaper, magazine, etc. is produced in 版本
23. **object** /ˈɔbdʒikt/ *n.* the purpose, aim, or goal of a specific action or effort 目的；目标
24. **watchdog** /ˈwɔtʃdɔg/ *n.* one who serves as a guardian against waste, loss, or illegal practices 监督者
25. **regulate** /ˈregjuleit/ *v.* to control an activity or process, especially by rules 规范；调控
26. **swear** /swɛə/ *v.* to curse 咒骂
27. **restriction** /risˈtrikʃən/ *n.* a rule or law that limits or controls what people can do 约束；限定
28. **Radio Corporation of America** 美国无线电公司
29. **corporation** /ˌkɔːpəˈreiʃən/ *n.* a company or a group of companies acting together as a single organization 公司
30. **telegram** /ˈteligræm/ *n.* a message transmitted by telegraph 电报
31. **broadcast** /ˈbrɔːdkɑːst/ *v.* to send out (a radio or television program) for public or general use 广播
32. **National Broadcasting Company** (美国)国家广播公司
33. **headquarters** /ˈhedˈkwɔːtəz/ *n.* a center of operations or administration 总部
34. **Columbia Broadcasting System** (美国)哥伦比亚广播公司
35. **live** /laiv/ *adj.* (of broadcasting) seen or heard as it happens 现场直播的
36. **symphony** /ˈsimfəni/ *n.* a long piece of music usually in four parts written for an orchestra 交响乐
37. **orchestra** /ˈɔːkistrə/ *n.* a large group of musicians playing many different kinds of instruments and led by a conductor 管弦乐队
38. **comedy** /ˈkɔmidi/ *n.* entertainment intended to make people laugh 喜剧
39. **Great Depression** (economic recession in America from 1929—1933)经济大萧条
40. **American Broadcasting Company** 美国广播公司
41. **break away from** (*phrasal verb*) to leave a group and form

another group, usually because of disagreement 脱离

42. **host** /həust/ *n.* someone who introduces and talks to the guests on a TV or radio program（男）主持人
43. **National Public Radio** （美国）国家公共电台
44. **American Public Radio** 美国公共电台
45. **charge** /tʃɑːdʒ/ *v.* to demand payment as a price 索价
46. **tune** /tjuːn/ *v.* to adjust a receiver so as to receive a particular signal 拨收；收听
47. **studio** /ˈstjuːdiəu/ *n.* a film company 电影公司
48. **merge** /məːdʒ/ *v.* to combine 合并
49. **United Paramount Theatres** 联合环球剧院
50. **paramount** /ˈpærəmaunt/ *adj.* supreme in rank, power, or authority 至高无上的
51. **Hollywood** /ˈhɔliwud/ *n.* the American motion-picture industry in the district of Los Angeles 好莱坞
52. **give way to** (*phrasal verb*) to yield to 屈服于
53. **sit-coms** /ˈsit-kɔms/ *n.* situation comedies 情景喜剧
54. **the ratings** a list that shows which films, television programs, etc. are the most popular 排名榜；等级
55. **household** /ˈhaushəuld/ *n.* the people who live together in one house 一户人；家庭
56. **Fox Broadcasting** 福克斯广播公司
57. **cable** /ˈkeibl/ *n.* a strong, large-diameter, heavy steel or fiber rope 电缆
58. **channel** /ˈtʃænl/ *n.* a TV station and all the programs that it broadcasts 电视频道
59. **Cable News Network** (CNN) 美国有线新闻网络
60. **immorality** /ˌiməˈræliti/ *n.* the state of being morally wrong 不道德
61. **recommend** /ˌrekəˈmend/ *v.* to suggest somebody or something good for a particular purpose 推荐
62. **guideline** /ˈgaidlain/ *n.* rules or instructions about the best way to do something 指导路线；方针

63. **critic** /'krɪtɪk/ *n.* someone who criticizes a person, organization or idea 批评家
64. **thoughtful** /'θɔːtful/ *adj.* seriously and carefully thought about 仔细思考的;深思熟虑的
65. **concerned** /kən'səːnd/ *adj.* involved in something or affected by it 关心的;有关的
66. **decline** /dɪ'klaɪn/ *n.* a decrease in quality, quantity, or importance of something 衰退
67. **outcome** /'aʊtkʌm/ *n.* the final result of a meeting, discussion, war, etc. 结果

Content Questions

1. What happens to a publisher if he publishes something that hurts another person?
2. Why are there print media in American society?
3. Why are newspapers and magazines sold very cheaply in America?
4. What do you learn about the United States Government as one of the largest publishers in the United States?
5. Who can influence what will be printed in newspapers and magazines?
6. Why did the late President Richard Nixon resign?
7. What kind of newspapers is read nationwide and how are local newspapers delivered?
8. Why are monthly magazines women-oriented and which monthly magazine has had the most readers?
9. Why are newspapers so important according to Thomas Jefferson, America's third President?
10. What can't the government do with broadcasting media? And what can it do?
11. According to broadcast media, who is responsible to improve society?

12. What do the opponents think broadcast media should do?
13. Why can't American government operate a radio or TV station to reach American people?
14. What are the three commercial networks in the United States and which one was established first?
15. What is the present situation of radio networks in the United States?
16. What impact did television have on radio and movie theaters?
17. How do broadcasters earn money in America?
18. Why were the years 1954 to 1959 the "Golden Years of Television"?
19. What did TV begin to reflect when color was brought to television?
20. What are the four major TV networks in the United States?
21. Why is Southern California a wonderful place to make movies?
22. What kind of movies became popular after World War II?
23. Why did Americans no longer regularly go to movies by the late 1990s?
24. What problems does TV bring and how can the problems be solved?
25. What are the benefits that TV brings and what is the basic disagreement?

Questions for Thinking and Discussion

1. Are there any differences between newspapers in China and those in America?

2. Are there any similarities between the TV programs in China and those in America?

3. What responsibilities do you think mass media should carry?

Test Paper

Part I True or False Statements

Directions: *The following statements are based on the passages in "**British and American Cultures and Customs**". Please read and see whether each of the statements is True or False according to what you have learned from the passages. Write **T** or **F** on the left of each statement.* (10%)

1. Americans' casual wear and behavior in routine life best display their characteristic of informality.   [**Unit One**]

2. You'd better not to ask people in the Western countries such questions as marriage, status, income, religious belief, or choice of voting, etc. [**Unit One**]

3. The British do not expect or welcome bargaining because they consider it insensitive and offensive.   [**Unit One**]

4. Americans do not expect you to show your courtesy in return, for they are understanding and enjoy welcoming you and feel pleased if you accept their friendship easily.   [**Unit Two**]

5. A host/hostess usually offers additional serving to the guests by passing the dish containing food from one person to another. [**Unit Two**]

6. Americans' preference to splitting the check fully indicates their stinginess.   [**Unit Two**]

7. The relationship of the individuals of the opposite sex may lead to casual acquaintance, a type of friendship or a passionate involvement or even marriage. 〔Unit Two〕

8. Both of the boy (man) and the girl (woman) in America have the responsibility for the expenses on the date. 〔Unit Two〕

9. You may miss smiles and brief conversations with people in the American cities where everyone appears in a hurry. 〔Unit Three〕

10. As Americans live in a mobile and ever-changing society in which people tend to avoid deep involvements with others, they tend to have casual friendship. 〔Unit Three〕

11. When struggling for their status and wealth, Americans usually ignore the spiritual or human aspect of life. 〔Unit Three〕

12. Driving in the U.S. entails not only mechanical manipulations of an automobile, but customary styles of driving. 〔Unit Three〕

13. People of all classes in Britain prefer to go to pub, in which they will have great fun and free talk in their private hours. 〔Unit Three〕

14. Restaurants on campus and on the outskirts of towns attract students, drivers and motorists because they are convenient and serve large portion of good and filling food at low prices. 〔Unit Four〕

15. The English people tend to underrate their own food and slight their cookery because their national cuisine is simple and awful. 〔Unit Four〕

16. The English enthusiastic adoption of foreign food has enriched their cuisine, and they have almost made some foreign food national dishes.   [**Unit Four**]

17. The tradition of holding an " Open House" on New Year's Day was brought into America by Dutch immigrants and the customs of dressing up in special costumes for New Year's Day parade and eating baked ham were brought by Swedish immigrants. [**Unit Five**]

18. The rules for the game of Easter Egg Roll are:
    a) To see who can roll an egg the longest time.
    b) To see who can make the egg roll without breaking it on a rough and windy road.   [**Unit Five**]

19. Americans' interest in spectator sports seems really excessive and even obsessive to many foreign visitors.   [**Unit Six**]

20. The American government is not allowed to operate a radio or TV station to reach American people, because American people fear that the government might take the advantage of media to influence voters in elections.   [**Unit Six**]

Part II Vocabulary

Directions: *There are 20 incomplete sentences in this part. For each sentence there are three choices. Choose the one that best completes the sentence. Then circle the corresponding letter you think is the right choice.* (10%)

1. A person's privacy is viewed as an individual _____ or private property that no one can share without permission in the U. S.
   A. possession   B. boundary   C. territory

2. "Avoiding excess at the dinner table" is viewed as "_____",

which is the hallmark of the common people in the Western world.

A. certainty   B. modesty   C. courtesy

3. In the United States, there is a widespread practice of making "small talk" in certain social situations. Small talk deals with various topics _____, simply for the sake of keeping a conversation going.

A. potentially   B. superficially   C. essentially

4. Americans do not show visitors great _____ of special courtesy if doing so requires much of their time.

A. amount   B. quantity   C. number

5. In America, dating a _____ of members of opposite sex does not indicate frivolity on part of a man or promiscuity on part of a woman.

A. category   B. variety   C. type

6. City people in America always appear in a hurry and tend to be impatient if they are delayed even for a _____ moment. They lead a fast paced life.

A. chief   B. certain   C. brief

7. The notable characteristics: Individualism, Informality, Casual Friendship, Time Consciousness, and Materialism best describe _____ and practices that are common among the American people.

A. attitudes   B. responses   C. impressions

8. On the arrival in the U. S., a foreign student should gain further information on local housing _____, and some knowledge of types of housing, rent, utilities, facilities, transit service, etc.

before signing a contract.

A. operations   B. options   C. organizations

9. Traffic accidents in the U. S. are usually considered to _____ carelessness, or mechanical failures, and not from "fate", "God's will", or other forces beyond human control.

A. coincide with   B. result from   C. get through

10. A great number of colorful foreign words have been brought into the English language, and many foreign dishes have _____ been adopted and anglicized since the Great Britain's colonial time.

A. constantly   B. continually   C. gradually

11. The Chinese woman found that eating American meals most _____. She could neither appreciate the food prepared by the Americans nor understand Americans' talk and laugh after the dinner.

A. troublesome   B. disturbing   C. elaborate

12. A New Year's resolution is a _____ to yourself to improve in some way in the coming new year.

A. dedication   B. determination   C. demonstration

13. Easter is now a festival less _____ and people in the Western countries celebrate it just for fun and enjoy it with the Easter Symbols—Easter Bunny, Easter Egg, and Easter flowers.

A. tedious   B. fabulous   C. religious

14. On Halloween night, people dress up in different costumes, wear _____, and yell "trick or treat!" at the doors of their neighbors' houses.

A. masks   B. jewels   C. ornaments

15. Sports and recreation absorb a huge amount of Americans' emotion, as well as their time, and _____, money.

    A. at any rate	B. in some cases	C. to some extent

16. Making noise while eating is considered as ill-bred, and a person who does so may _____ those who are having dinner with him/her.

    A. bother	B. restrict	C. offend

17. When invited to a dinner, you should not express your _____ or dislike of certain foods. Either eat it or pass it over quietly. Eat it if you like and set it aside if you dislike it.

    A. displeasure	B. disapproval	C. disregard

18. When purchasing a car, it is _____ for the foreign student to be accompanied by an American who is familiar with the procedures involved, price ranges, and so forth.

    A. advisable	B. adequate	C. acceptable

19. The most refined action of "please pass me the salt/pepper." is not about the _____ but requires the greatest number of steps to carry it out.

    A. sufficiency	B efficiency	C. frequency

20. President Nixon had to resign mainly because reporters for Washington Post newspaper _____ that the president had lied when he was asked about the Watergate burglary.

    A. reflected	B. released	C. revealed

Part III Translation

Directions: *There are 10 incomplete sentences in this part. In each sentence there are two blanks for you to fill in with appropriate English words with the reference of the Chinese words given in the bracket. Please write your translation on each line. (10%)*

1. A self-introduction is _____ _____ （一般足以） to gain acceptance into a group or join in a conversation in the U. S. 〔**Unit One**〕

2. People's behavior in public places, like their behavior anywhere else, is _____（易于受到）to cultural _____（影响）. 〔**Unit Two**〕

3. The goal of gaining core knowledge of table manners is to behave with _____（谦和）and _____（沉着）at the dinner table. 〔**Unit Two**〕

4. Living with a host family temporarily is one of the housing options for a foreign student before he/she finds a suitable and _____ _____（永久的住处）. 〔**Unit Three**〕

5. Americans are always ready to move because they are _____（不安分）and try to _____（追求）something new and better. 〔**Unit Three**〕

6. The Chinese woman feels an _____（反感）to the American fast food, such as hot dogs, hamburgers, and sandwiches, because they are all _____（无味）and smell worse. 〔**Unit Four**〕

7. In the past, when kids rang the doorbell, people inside the house were _____（期望/就得）to come out and give _____（夸赞）to the kids' costumes and put some coins into the "trick or treat"

bags. 〖Unit Five〗

8. The German immigrants bought the _____ (象征物) of the Easter Bunny to America. It was widely _____ (忽略) by other Christians until shortly after the Civil War. 〖Unit Five〗

9. Although some recreational activities are costly and time and _____ _____ (精力消耗), most Americans think they are worthwhile. 〖Unit Six〗

10. The sports ethic is expressed in the Olympic Creed, which is not to win but to take part, just as the most important thing in life is not the _____ (成功的喜悦) but the _____ (拼搏). 〖Unit Six〗

Part IV Questions

Directions: *Please give a brief answer to each of the following questions according to what you have learned from* ***British and American Cultures and Customs***. *Write your answers under each question.* (10%)

1. What do the Westerners think of the Chinese students' excessive expression of gratitude and what is overdoing apology actually considered in the Western world? 〖Unit One〗

2. What does the notion "Line up, and wait your turn." reflect? 〖Unit Two〗

3. What is the definition of "Dutch treat"? 〖Unit Two〗

4. Why is American society said to "be ruled by the clock"? 〖Unit Three〗

5. Why does a foreign student have to pay a deposit before moving into an apartment or a house? 〖Unit Three〗

6. Where do middle class people in Britain prefer to go to spend their leisure hours and why?　**[Unit Three]**

7. Why is the United States described as a "melting pot"?　**[Unit Four]**

8. What do people usually do on April Fool's Day?　**[Unit Five]**

9. What are the features of Thanksgiving Day?　**[Unit Five]**

10. Why is it said that sports business is a big business in America? **[Unit Six]**

Part V　Writing

Directions: *In this part there are two topics "**The Chinese Spring Festival**"/"**The Chinese New Year**" and "**Stress in Life**". Choose one of the topics and write an essay within 200 words. Please write your composition neatly on the paper..* (10%)

A. Write something about the customs and habits Chinese people have on **"The Spring Festival/ The Chinese New Year"** and describe how Chinese celebrate this traditional holiday.

B. Write an essay about **"Stress in Life"**
   a) What are the sources of your stress and pressure in life?
   b) What are the positive and negative effects of stress and pressure?
   c) What solutions you may take to minimize your stress in life?

Answers

Part I True or False Statements （10%）
1. T   2. T   3. F   4. T   5. F
6. F   7. T   8. F   9. T   10. T
11. F 12. T 13. F 14. T 15. F
16. T 17. T 18. F 19. T 20. T

Part II Vocabulary （10%）
1. C   2. B   3. B   4. A   5. B
6. C   7. A   8. B   9. B   10. C
11. A 12. B 13. C 14. A 15. B
16. C 17. B 18. A 19. B 20. C

Part III Translation （10%）
1. normally, sufficient
2. subject, influence
3. graciousness/gracefulness, poise
4. permanent, residence
5. restless, pursue
6. aversion, tasteless
7. expected/supposed, praise/compliment
8. symbol, ignored
9. energy, consuming
10. triumph, struggle

Part IV Questions （10%）
1. empty thanks and insincerity, an awkward behavior
2. People are all equal and no one has the privilege of going directly to the front of a line. /American people's aversion to touching and

being touched.
3. Split the check /share the expenses/pay one's own expenses
4. Everything is done in orderly fashion or by means of schedule. / People are expected to be punctual.
5. for the damages during one's occupancy/ It will be available for the repair.
6. To saloon bars, which are more comfortable and less crowded.
7. Because of its diversity. /Because it consists of different cultures, nationalities, beliefs and so on.
8. They play practical jokes/tricks on other people/They make good clean fun of other people without hurting/ insulting/harming them.
9. Family (reunion), feast, football and friends
10. Sports games require clothing, supplies, equipments that can be quite costly/surprisingly expensive, and some companies make big profits by advertising their products on TV, newspapers, magazines, etc.

Part V Writing (10%)

Directions: *In this part there are two topics "The Spring Festival"/"The Chinese New Year" and "Stress in Life." Choose one of the topics and write an essay within 200 words. Please write your composition neatly the paper.* (10%)

A. Write something about the customs and habits Chinese people have on the **"The Spring Festival"/"The Chinese New Year"** and describe how Chinese celebrate this traditional holiday.

B. Write an essay about **"Stress in Life"**
   a) What are the sources of your stress and pressure in life?
   b) What are the positive and negative effects of stress and pressure?
   c) What are solutions you can find to minimize stress in life?